Hudson Taylor

God's Man for China

Hudson Taylor
God's Man for China

BETTY MACINDOE

HODDER AND STOUGHTON
LONDON SYDNEY AUCKLAND TORONTO

Contents

CHAPTER ONE

"I'm going to be a missionary"

HUDSON WRIGGLED UNCOMFORTABLY. Escape seemed impossible. He could feel the man's arm tightening around his waist. His legs dangled helplessly a few inches from the ground. This was an unexpected turn of events and to him every minute was agony. He had come into the sitting-room to say "Goodnight" to his parents before going upstairs for he had a plan to put into operation and was in a hurry to get to his room. But a friend who was visiting the home on that chilly winter evening had offered to tell him a story, and before he could protest, he was a prisoner on the visitor's knee.

He sat up straight and sniffed gently in the direction of the huge log fire. Could he detect the smell of melting wax? He did not dare put his hand into his jacket-pocket. He could only imagine what was happening. He was sure that any moment now the liquid wax from the candle-ends which he had hidden there would ooze out and form a blob on the carpet. He squinted down but, as far as he could see, there was nothing unusual happening. The story-teller went on and on. Hudson waited for a break.

At last, a pause. It was his chance.

"May I be excused now? It is really past my bedtime."

He tried to break away. But no. Mother was too quick for him, saying that he could stay up for a bit longer tonight as a special favour! He felt the visitor tug him a bit closer. It only made him more fidgety and miserable. His carefully-laid scheme was going all wrong.

That day he had searched in all the odd corners of the kitchen and the cellar for the stump-ends of candles, stuffing all he could find into his pocket ready for use. His mother usually came into his room at night and took away the oil-lamp when it was time for him to go to sleep. Tonight, when she had gone, he meant to light the candle-ends one by one so that he could enjoy a long, reading session. He had found a very exciting book on one of the shelves, but with lessons and mealtimes he never had time to get down to it. Now the hot fire and the visitor's story were spoiling everything.

It seemed ages before the story came to an end. Hudson jumped up, free at last.

"Goodnight, everybody," he called out hurriedly and fled from the room and upstairs. Nervously he felt in his pocket. It was too late. The candle-ends had merged into an unusable mess. Angry and disappointed, he flung himself on to his bed and burst into tears. Grown-ups do have a way of ruining things, he thought, as he sobbed.

Minutes later his mother was in the room beside him.

"What's wrong, Hudson?" she asked, puzzled at his behaviour downstairs.

It was so unlike him not to want to hear a story and so unusual for him to want to go to bed early! Hudson knew that there was no point in pretending to be unwell or making any other excuses. His mother had a way of finding out anyway. So he told her the whole story. She listened but did not say very much. Then quietly she turned down the wick and took the lamp out of the room.

He lay in the darkness, wondering. Would she tell Father? He hoped not. Mr Taylor was very

very strict and, when he scolded, his loud sharp voice made Hudson quake. Father would not stand for any kind of disobedience or bad behaviour. His set of rules were to be obeyed without any questions, and sometimes when Hudson or his sister, Amelia, did something wrong, Father punished them severely. Hudson dreaded the morning.

When he got up he washed his face and tidied his hair before appearing at the breakfast table — that was one of his father's stipulations. He was there in good time too, for that was another unbreakable rule. "If there are five people," his father would say, "and they are kept waiting for one minute, do you not see that five minutes are lost that can never be found again?"

But breakfast went off happily. When he had finished his porridge and bread-and-butter and not a word about last night had been spoken, Hudson knew that all was well. Now he could concentrate on his programme of lessons for the day.

Lessons for him did not mean going to school. Although Mr Taylor could probably have afforded to send him to boarding-school, Hudson was never well enough to be sent away from home for very long. His longest stretch away at school lasted for only a matter of months. Besides, Mr Taylor was not one to spend money unnecessarily! So he organised lessons at home, with Mrs Taylor helping out in the afternoons.

Home was behind and above Father's chemist-shop which faced on to the cobbled Market Square of Barnsley, a mining town in Yorkshire. When Hudson could not work out a mathematical problem, he simply slipped through the connecting door into the shop where his father in white jacket and apron measured out medicines for his customers. Mr Taylor was excellent at figures. He knew all about decimals and had made up his own system of logarithm tables. So he did not mind explaining things to Hudson.

And sometimes Hudson would sneak a few extra minutes in the shop just to watch his father at work. It was fascinating! He weighed every grain and counted every drop exactly. He knew where every bottle and every container were to be found. He wrote every label on the customers' prescriptions in clear handwriting. Nothing was ever too much trouble, yet he found time to chat with the people coming in from the country, to advise them about their sicknesses and to pass on a kindly greeting. He also made sure that no-one ever went without medicine because they did not have the money to pay for it right away.

In the afternoons Hudson joined Amelia for lessons under Mother's charge. While she did her sewing, the children read aloud to her. When Amelia stumbled over a long word, she made her go over it slowly till she could say it properly.

When Hudson did not know a meaning, he had to fetch the dictionary from the shelf and look up the word. They spent time on history and reading travel-stories, and Mother often made them write from her dictation.

There was not much change in the daily routine but Saturday afternoons were sometimes a bit more special. Mr Taylor shut the shop at noon and after lunch, if the weather was fine, he took Amelia and Hudson on long nature-trails when they had great fun together getting to know the countryside. Father seemed to know the name of every bird, tree, flower and butterfly, and supplied the children with all sizes of pill-boxes from the shop so that they could collect insect specimens and bring them home. He also bought a monthly magazine on natural history for them and they spent whole evenings studying it together.

Sundays were quite different. The Taylors were chapel people, Methodists. Attendance at morning service was an occasion, never to be missed. Mr Taylor, a deeply religious man, was frequently away from home taking the services in other chapels in the area. Hudson was sometimes allowed to go with him. He really loved to hear his father preach, and admired his vigorous style, his loud, booming voice and his great knowledge.

It was quite an event too when visiting preachers came to their home in Barnsley. Three or four times a year a business meeting was held in the Barnsley chapel and when it was over, there would be a delicious meal on the big dining-table in the Taylor home with lots of talk and laughter. Somehow Father always managed to turn the conversation round to his favourite topic — the work of the Church overseas. Hudson would sit in his place quite unnoticed by the adults, listening avidly to all their lively discussion.

"Now, why don't we send missionaries *there*?" Mr Taylor asked his usual question, referring to China in which he had a very great interest. He had studied all he could about this land of charm and mystery which sent its cargoes of silks and jade and tea to the west. And he knew that missionaries were few in China and their work was limited to five coastal towns. He even suggested a scheme for sending thousands of Bibles immediately into the land so that all who could read should have a free copy. His proposal sounded very convincing to Hudson.

It was after one of those mealtimes, when Father had made his point again, that suddenly a small voice piped up,

"When I am a man, I mean to be a missionary and go to China." It was Hudson. Everyone stared at him in surprise, and maybe a little amusement. But no one discouraged him.

CHAPTER TWO

The Gospel Tract

HUDSON PULLED OUT a handkerchief and patted his red eyes for they stung like mad. Soon he would be going home, leaving the hard wooden stool and the high desk at the bank where he worked as a clerk. It was already quite late and the dim gaslight was no help to his eyes as he wrote up the day's takings in the massive ledger.

"Sorry you're leaving us, Taylor," one of the other juniors was saying.

"Couldn't be more sorry than I am," Hudson

replied and tried to add a laugh. He really hated
having to give up his good job in one of the best
banks in town, a job for which there had been a
long list of applicants, but his eyes could not take
the strain any longer. He was very disappointed.
He had made up his mind to become rich, own a
grand house and a fine horse and have the chance
to ride out with the hunt. How often he had pic-
tured himself in the colourful red gear of the
huntsman! After all, that was considered *the*
thing in 1849. He had had good times too with the
other boys in the bank. At sixteen, what else was
there to think about but balls and girls and the gay
life? It was all so appealing. But now he had to go
home.

Home! How dull it seemed now! Amelia was
good fun really, but she was so shocked if he said
anything out-of-place. Besides, she was going off
to boarding-school after the summer holidays.
Father just could not understand him any more,
of that he was sure, for he had given him a beating
just for letting out a swear word. Mother was
usually very patient with him and he could trust
her, but she could be insistent too. Well, he would
have to face it all. But the thing he most dreaded
was having to earn his living helping Father in
the shop.

Yet shop-life had its moments, Hudson had to
admit: faces peering in at the window; the

'clobbing' of clogs on the cobbles; the bargain-shouters in the market-place; the wheezy old men and the gossiping women who paid regular calls. During the day he discovered it was not too bad apart from the washing out of countless medicine bottles. But in the evenings when he tried to get some study done, how often Hudson's mind wandered off to his friends from the bank and their pleasures which he was no longer allowed to share! Why were his family so narrow in their thinking and so plain in their way of living? Could they not exchange some of that for some gaiety and pleasure? The only entertainment the Taylors indulged in was musical evenings. Hudson played the flute very well and he had not a bad singing voice and together the family formed a group of sorts, but their themes were mostly religious.

Hudson felt a fraud. He did not know if he even believed in God any more. How shocked his parents would be if he ever whispered as much! Amelia was just like Mother, very sure of what she believed. *He* knew better now, decidedly, for his time in the bank had opened his eyes. He was embarrassed too by the Sunday walk to chapel when he was so conspicuous in his tailored suit and his sandy-red hair. The routine of prayers, hymn-singing and chapel was getting him down.

One half-closing day he was really fed up.

Father was having a rest and Mother had gone off for a couple of weeks to visit some friends, and Amelia was nowhere to be seen. Hudson was bored! Here he was on this fine summer afternoon with no friends of his own age with whom he could go out. He wandered aimlessly into his father's library and looked at the shelves. He picked out a book, thumbed through its pages and put it back. He chose another and did the same again. There was nothing there to interest him. He looked around the room. On the table was a basketful of small paper-covered booklets, 'Gospel tracts' they were called. Hudson knew exactly what their line was — a story with a moral tacked on at the end. They all followed the same pattern. He flicked through the pile and picked one out, deciding to read the story-section and skip the rest. He found a corner in the warehouse at the back of the property and settled down to read.

"Hm, I wonder what that means?" Hudson spoke the words half-aloud. He had come to the 'moral' part of the story and was still reading! He had just come across the words 'the finished work of Christ' and could get no further. With his finger still at the page, he closed the book and sat thinking. He remembered another phrase which was something the same.

"Jesus said, 'It is finished' when he was on the cross and about to die," thought Hudson.

As he sat there the two phrases began to mean something. In a few seconds it all became clear to him — Jesus had done everything, that was why His was a 'finished work'. Jesus had died and was alive again to prove it. And since Jesus had done everything there was nothing more to do, he reasoned. That was absolutely tremendous. But wait, there was just one thing for him to do.

"Get on your knees and thank God," he thought he heard a voice saying to him, and he did just that in the corner of the darkening warehouse. He asked for complete forgiveness for all his past doubtings and sin. The relief he felt as he got up was beyond words. The days of pretending and of double-living were over, and he was glad. He no longer needed to act the Christian. He knew he was one.

He was more sure than ever three days later when he could keep his secret no longer and decided to tell Amelia.

"Amelia," he called, and when she came he asked her,

"Will you promise not to tell anyone else if I tell you something?"

Amelia nodded her curly head. She was flattered at being asked to share her big brother's confidences. "I'll not tell a soul. I promise you I shan't."

Hudson did his best to explain what had happened in the warehouse and Amelia threw up her arms in delight and hugged him. This was the very news which she had been longing for. Then she explained that, unknown to Hudson, she had been praying three times every day for the past six weeks for something like this to happen to him. And now it had!

In two weeks' time Mother came back home again. Hudson rushed to meet her at the door.

"Mother, I've got news for you," he blurted out at once.

"Yes, I know you have," she replied excitedly.

"How do you know? Has Amelia broken her promise? She said she would tell no-one!" Hudson sounded a bit upset.

"No, Amelia hasn't told me anything. I just know." And Mrs Taylor went on to explain to him how, two weeks before, while on holiday and in her room alone one afternoon, she had felt an urge to pray for Hudson. After two hours in prayer she knew that God had not only heard her prayer but had already answered. She knew that Hudson had made his very big decision. It was almost unbelievable!

Now that they had found a new united and happy relationship, Hudson and Amelia put their heads together and thought up ways of helping other people. For the rest of that summer they were busy visiting old people in their homes, bringing what happiness they could to poor people who stayed at the lodging-houses, and gave out Gospel leaflets around the race-course.

Then, all of a sudden, Amelia went off to school in Barton and Hudson found himself dreadfully alone, which was bad enough. But on top of that he had to share his room with cousin John, who had come to work in the shop. John was a tease and made fun of Hudson when he saw him reading his Bible and praying at night or in the mornings. It was too much. Hudson slackened off his Bible reading and prayers and misery got into his being. The one bright spot was when Amelia came home and brought her music teacher with her whom she introduced to the family. Hudson thought her attractive and rather sweet.

But then they had gone again and his misery returned. He wanted desperately to make progress in his Christian living, but, when John was around, his courage disappeared. He was making no headway at all. Feeling desperate, he asked God to do something special for him. He did not know what exactly, but he made a bargain with God. On his knees he told God that if He did something for him, he would give God all of his life in return. A voice, heard by Hudson if by no-one else, said to him there and then,

"Then go for me to China."

To China? Was he dreaming? Was he imagining? No. God had said that he was to go to China. What a thought! From now on he would have to prepare.

First he managed to borrow a book on China from the local Congregational minister, and then another friend produced a Chinese Bible in the Mandarin dialect. His language-study was not very brilliant as he had no teacher and had to make guesses at words, but he learned all he could about the land. He tried in other ways to get ready too. He went for long walks on the windswept moors to build up his stamina. He toughened his body by giving up sleeping on a feather bed, and he took lessons in theology, Greek and Latin. But his chief study was medicine, for he was sure that it would be most useful to him in later years.

CHAPTER THREE

How Hudson was paid his Wages

"POSTMAN, MR TAYLOR!"

Mrs Finch, the landlady, came into Hudson's room, her wet hands grasping an envelope in the folds of her apron. Hudson looked at the blurred postmark.

"I wonder who this is from, and on a Monday morning too?"

He tore it open. Someone had sent him a pair of expensive-looking gloves. He pulled them out from their wrapping. Oops! Something bright fell out also. A gleaming half-sovereign! Who had sent this? There was no letter inside. No address on the outside. Funny! Then he burst out laughing.

"Four hundred per cent interest! That's pretty good going. Half-a-crown invested in God's bank for twelve hours has brought me in half-a-sovereign!"

He laughed again at the memory of that last half-crown piece which he had parted company with the night before. It was the only coin he had in the world because his employer, Dr Hardey, had forgotten to pay him. He had fumbled it around in his pocket before he could bring himself to give it away. After the mission service a man had pleaded with him to visit his attic room where his wife was seriously ill. He said he wanted the young preacher to pray for her. Hudson was terribly shocked to find a family of hungry, crying children with no food in the cupboard. So his precious piece had gone, and all he had in *his* cupboard was enough oatmeal for two bowlfuls of porridge.

He looked again at the half-sovereign and felt terribly happy. It was a thrill to realise that God must have known his state of affairs and had made some unknown friend post an envelope with money in it to him in time to arrive before he left for work. Yet he had never told anyone but God about his poverty. Now he had proved that he need never tell anyone else but God. He could trust God to make other people do His business by just praying that He would. For Hudson, from that moment, a new way of life began. Now he could pray with confidence that God would remind Dr Hardey that his salary was already over-due, and see results.

Dr Hardey was a relative in Hull to whom Hudson had come to do medical training. At first he had lodged with the doctor's family, then had moved out to stay with an aunt. Finally he had decided to rent a room on one of the poorest quarters of the town so that he could live more cheaply, give more away, help the needy people of the area and so prepare a bit more for life abroad. He found Mrs Finch, who was glad to have him in her spare room in her end-terrace house.

His half-sovereign lasted for almost two weeks as Hudson's diet was mainly brown biscuits and herring, but when Saturday came again, he was in a fix. He still had not been paid his salary. His rent was due and Mrs Finch could do with the money, but he was penniless. Should he say something to Dr Hardey? No, he would go on praying.

Late Friday afternoon he was in the surgery tidying up for the weekend. Dr Hardey had just finished writing up his prescription forms when suddenly he sat back in his armchair and in a casual voice said, "Oh, by the way, Taylor, isn't your salary due again?"

Fortunately for Hudson his back was to the doctor. He stirred the mixture he was boiling in a pan carefully and swallowed hard before telling the doctor as politely as possible that he should have been paid some time before. The good doctor apologised and scolded Hudson for not reminding him sooner. Then he went on,

"I'm so sorry, for only this afternoon I sent all the money I had to the bank."

Again it was a good thing that Hudson was busy at that moment! The mixture boiled up and he rushed with it out of the room, his feelings rather like the concoction — all up at the top and ready to boil over! A second or two before, he was sure that God had kept His part of the deal, but now the prospect was bleak for the weekend. No money for himself was grim enough, but none for Mrs Finch ... He could not believe it. He only hoped that all would be put right on Monday.

When the doctor had gone over to his house, Hudson stayed. He finished his work and spent some time in the warmth of the surgery, reading his Bible and preparing for the Sunday services at the lodging-houses. It was about ten o'clock when he finally decided to pack up for the night. He put his coat on and was just about to turn out the gas when he thought he heard footsteps on the path outside. He looked out and saw Dr Hardey was coming back, laughing his head off!

"Can you imagine it? One of my patients has decided to pay his bill at this hour of night! Why on earth should he do that? He could have paid by cheque at any hour of the day. Yet he came with cash now. What an odd thing!"

The doctor laughed again as he entered the amount into his receipt book and Hudson enjoyed the joke with him. Then the doctor turned to go again. On a sudden impulse he thrust his hand into Hudson's and left a wad of notes there.

"You might as well take these, Taylor. I'll give you the balance of your salary next week."

Hudson squeezed the precious papers in the palm of his hand. If only the doctor had known what they meant to him! He was more sure than ever that God wanted him in China, and that He would look after him there just as He had done right at that moment.

CHAPTER FOUR

The lone Voyager

SAILS FLAPPED NOISILY in the breeze. Masts creaked and groaned. The *Dumfries* slowly nosed her way through the Liverpool dock gates. But who could that be up in the rigging? Surely not a sailor in frock-coat and topper! The fellow could be seen swaying backwards and forwards, gripping the rope-ladder in one hand and waving his hat in the other. It was Hudson Taylor on his way at last to China!

It had been an awful ordeal for him to say

'goodbye' to his mother. They had prayed together in his cabin, then she had gone ashore and sat down on a pile of timber on the quayside. She had looked so upset that he had run down the gangplank to give her a final hug. Then, as the ship was moving out, he had quickly pencilled a message on the blank page of a small Bible which he tossed over to her. The words reminded her of God's love, and he knew they would be a comfort. Now, as the dock gates opened to allow the ship through into the open sea, Hudson waved frantically from his perch till his mother's white handkerchief became a tiny fading speck in the distance. Then he went below to unpack some of his belongings, the only passenger on board, with a voyage of almost six months ahead.

Six months! And on this small ship! What a prospect! He would know every plank and every rope on her by then, he thought. But before six days had passed, a violent storm threatened to wreck both the ship and his missionary career. Gale-force winds battered the sails and strained the timbers. A furious sea poured over the sides The ship climbed the breakers and plunged terrifyingly into the depths in a storm which alarmed even the captain and his crew. Poor Hudson! He was much more used to the countryside and the thought of being drowned was quite frightening.

On and on, for days the storm raged. The ship

was driven dangerously near the rocks off the coast of Wales. Hudson even unpacked one of his hampers with the idea of using it as a sort of raft if the ship broke up. Then he wrote his name and address into his diary and fastened it inside his clothing so that he could be identified if picked up. At twenty-one years of age he wondered if this was to be the end of everything for him, and he did not like the idea too much. Alone in his cabin he looked up some verses in his Bible, and knelt to pray. Then he felt God was very close to him and was promising him safety and courage. Feeling much better, he was able to go on deck.

"Do you think we can clear Holyhead?" he asked the captain anxiously.

"If we make no lee-way, we may just do it," was the worried man's answer. "But if we drift, God help us!"

The water was white with foam, the land nearer than ever and the ship made no progress.

"We must try to turn her and tack," the captain decided, "or all is lost."

He gave the orders swiftly and the men put all their strength into turning the ship, but it was useless. Then, at the last moment they tried the other way and succeeded. The ship cleared the rocks by yards. At that very moment the wind changed direction very slightly and they were safe. Hudson believed God had helped them.

The storm had been so bad that weeks later Hudson's clothes still felt damp from the sea-water that had soaked through everything. It was horrible to have to put his feet into cold clammy shoes in the morning, but fortunately his books and his papers were not damaged badly.

In fact the long voyage was exactly what he needed. From working with Dr Hardey in Hull, he had moved to London where a year of medical studies exhausted him. Just imagine an eight-mile walk every day to the London Hospital and back to his lodgings on a diet of brown bread and apples! No wonder it proved too much for him. He thought that being tough on himself was good preparation for life in China, but instead it just pulled his health down so much that when a pricked finger became infected while he was working on a corpse, he nearly died. That illness put an end to his spartan ways of living.

Not only had he been very ill, he had been also very heartbroken. He had become engaged to his sister's music-teacher but her parents would not hear of her going abroad as a missionary and the engagement had been broken off.

It was good that he really was on his way to China at last — the land of which he had read and talked and dreamed for three years — and encouraging news had reached Britain of a change in Government there. A Christian Emperor who

had given his country the new title of *T'ai-ping,
T'ien-Kuo*, the Heavenly Kingdom of Great
Peace, was now in command. It seemed just the
right time to send missionaries out and when the
Chinese Evangelisation Society had put the question to him, Hudson was willing to give up his
studies at the London Hospital and go at once.
Besides, the Bible Society was printing a million
copies of the New Testament in the Mandarin
dialect so that they could be given away freely to
all who could read.

But he was to see only sea for weeks and
weeks — the Bay of Biscay, the Equator, the Cape
of Good Hope, the Indian Ocean. No mail, no
radio messages, no news of the outside world. The
Dumfries was a little world of her own, sailing
along day after day. But it gave Hudson plenty of
time for reading and study. His Bible became a
wonderful library. He had brought with him his
Latin and Greek readers, his books on natural history, piles of medical text-books as well as all the
books and papers he had managed to find on
China. As the ship sailed through tropical seas, he
spent many hours on deck under the clearest skies
he had ever seen, reading and daydreaming.
Sometimes he would gaze over the side into the
blue-bright waters and watch for tiny sea-creat-
ures, tracing their passage by their light trails.
When an albatross or a shark was caught he

joined in the excitement, but most of the time was quite uneventful and very peaceful.

Perhaps too peaceful. During long, hot days the ship scarcely made any progress through the Pacific Islands. It was only at sunset that a slight breeze rose and filled the sails, driving the vessel a little farther. It was on one of those days when they were headed north after passing New Guinea, that Hudson saw worry written all over the captain's face. He paced up and down the deck, looking first over one side of the ship and then over the other.

"Lower the long-boat," he shouted.

The crew obeyed at once and Hudson watched and wondered as the men attached ropes between the two boats and rowed for all they were worth.

"What are they doing?" he asked as he sauntered up to the captain.

"Trying to turn her head," said the captain without taking his eyes off what was happening. Then he explained that a powerful undercurrent was drawing the ship steadily towards a deadly sunken reef. After some time the men in the long-boat were exhausted and yet there was still no change in the ship's direction. The captain ordered them aboard, and began pacing the deck again.

"Well, we've done all we can. We must just wait

now." His voice sounded hopeless as he spoke to Hudson.

"No, there's something else we can do," was Hudson's quick reply as a thought flashed through his mind. The captain was curious.

"Let all of us who are Christians go to our cabins and pray. God can give us a breeze right now just as easily as at sunset."

The idea maybe sounded a bit odd, but the captain agreed and those who wanted to pray did so. It was not very long before Hudson was on deck again, giving orders to one of the officers to let down the corners of the mainsail. The officer thought he had gone crazy and was in no mood to take orders from a passenger anyway. But Hudson insisted and got his way.

"Look. Look, up there!" he shouted, shading his eyes with one hand and pointing with the other.

Sure enough the limp tiny sail at the top of the highest mast was beginning to shiver. Within seconds every hand was on deck, sails were hoisted, ropes let out. The wind had come and was driving them away from danger at some speed.

Prayer to God had worked another miracle. One young man was never to forget his first voyage to China for once again by what happened he learned to trust God in difficult situations. In the years ahead he was going to have to trust God many more times in the same way.

CHAPTER FIVE

Alone and penniless in Shanghai

FROM THE BOW of their brown-sailed sampan, the boatmen glanced suspiciously at the stranger. Their passenger must surely be a foreign devil, they thought, for all devils had red hair! But his spectacles and his serious face made him look more like a teacher. Hudson wrapped his warm coat a bit closer around him for it was a cold February day. He knew that they were discussing him at the other end of the boat, and he would have given anything to know what they were saying.

He would have loved it even more had he been able to join in their chatter, but they kept their distance all the fifteen miles up the Woosung creek to Shanghai.

For almost four days the *Dumfries* had lain fog-bound at the mouth of the Yangtse River. Hudson, all packed-up and ready to disembark, found this last-minute delay because of fog very frustrating. When the pilot finally came on board they moved slowly up the channel for only a short distance before they were forced to cast anchor again. Nor had this first visitor from shore brought very good news. England was on the verge of war, he told them. China was already in the grip of a cruel civil war with Imperialist and Rebel troops fighting bitterly. There was fighting even in Shanghai where stocks of food were down to famine level. Prices had rocketed and foreign money had little value.

It was a very gloomy picture, but somehow it did not seem to deter the new missionary. When his chance came to complete his voyage in the little wooden Chinese craft, he took it immediately. Now through the lifting fog, he distinguished the outline of the land and the buildings which meant only one thing.

Shanghai! Hudson stepped ashore, his heart beating wildly. This was the moment he had waited for. He almost cried with joy. Gripping his bags firmly, he hurried after his guide through the muddy streets, not daring to take his eyes off him, for all the men seemed so alike in their loose-fitting jackets and trousers of blue cotton. His first call was at the British Consulate to report his arrival. He had brought with him only a few belongings, his official papers and three very important letters from friends at home to people whom they knew in Shanghai. These people, they thought, might be able to help him get settled into his new life, and he was looking forward to meeting them.

Things did not turn out as he expected. At the Consulate no-one seemed very impressed that a young Englishman had arrived! No one had heard that he was coming. There was no mail waiting for him from home and no money from the Chinese Evangelisation Society, the group who had sent him out. Hudson could hardly believe it, for, as he had very little money of his own, the situation was grim. It became even worse when he learned that two of the people to whom his letters of introduction were addressed were no longer in Shanghai. One had died and the other had gone home to America. What about the third, he asked? Yes, Dr Medhurst was in the city. He lived in one of the houses of the London Missionary Society, right over at the other side of the Settlement (the non-Chinese part of Shanghai), the Chinese clerk told him. Then he bowed low, as he showed Hudson to the door, indicating the direction he should take.

As he set off he found new sights and sounds and smells everywhere. Shop-fronts lined the narrow streets. First-floor balconies jutted out, blocking the light. Curiously-worked signs indicating what each shop sold swung noisily overhead. Bowls of delicious-smelling food were displayed on street-stalls. Now and again the crowd would be elbowed back to allow a sedan chair to pass, then they would surge again into the street. It seemed to Hudson as if he were walking through the pages of the books he had read. But when he came in sight of a mission-chapel in the Shantung Road and saw the wide iron gateway of the London Mission Compound lying open, he knew it was real.

The gateman bowed to the visitor. Hudson showed him his letter of introduction and said smilingly,

"Dr Medhurst?"

"Doctor not at home. Doctor gone away," was the polite reply which left Hudson speechless, looking at the shaved head and the pigtail of the gateman as he bowed again.

He tried to continue the conversation, but the man's knowledge of English had obviously run out. At the sound of the voices, an inquisitive array of faces peeped from behind curtains. In no time at all a number had slipped quietly into the courtyard with the good intention of helping. But as one and another made signs and sounds, the chaos increased. The trouble was that they all wanted to speak at once, and not a word did Hudson understand.

It was all so puzzling now to him. Where should he go from here, he wondered? Should he try to make his way back to the *Dumfries* before nightfall? At least he would have a bunk there for the night and some food. How strange to think that he had come those thousands of miles to find neither a home nor a friend! As he stood there he prayed. At that moment, another door opened and a young man, dressed in European clothes, came across the yard.

"Hallo, I am Joseph Edkins," he said cheerily, holding out his hand. "Dr Medhurst is not here at the moment, but Dr Lockhart is. Do please come in . . ."

What a relief to hear someone say something he could understand! Hudson went in for tea and talk and a comfortable bed. In the morning he was awakened by a servant who brought him hot water for washing. It was so much better than he had imagined after all! He got up and looked out of the window. There in the garden the trees were budding and some were bursting into blossom.

Farther away green corn was waving in the fields. How good it was to be alive, he thought, and everything was going to be all right.

"I'll have to see about a language teacher right away," he said to himself as he shaved. "Then I'd better find out when the *Dumfries* is due to dock. I must call in again at the Consulate too just to check on mail and money."

At breakfast Dr Lockhart offered to find him an excellent Mandarin teacher. But a visit to the Consulate produced only one letter from his family. As soon as the *Dumfries* was in port, Hudson hired a number of coolies to transport his baggage to the Mission Compound. He laughed to see their conical, straw hats bobbing up and down to the rhythm of their jog-trot as single-file, his loads slung at the ends of bouncing bamboo poles, they made their way along the dockside and through the streets. As they went they chanted a warning call of "Ou-ah, Ou-ay" to let people know to clear the way. He was thrilled to be right there amongst those to whom God had sent him. He was just bursting to be able to speak to them.

CHAPTER SIX

The North Gate House

"YOU ASK ME how I get over my troubles, Amelia. This is the way. I take them to the Lord."

Hudson was writing one of his long letters to his sister. Summer heat made the perspiration run in trickles down his neck and over his collar. His moist hand stuck to the paper as he pushed his pen over it. But he enjoyed writing in great detail to his favourite sister for she wrote such marvellously lengthy letters in reply. Letters from home took at least three and a half months to come by the quickest route, and when they arrived he spent hours reading and re-reading every word. This really had a bad effect on him, for it made him dreadfully homesick. Then he would take his concertina out and play folk music to relieve his feelings. He was most disappointed when the mail brought no news from his Society who seemed to have forgotten about him altogether. This left him with real problems for he hardly knew how to make his money spin out. The missionaries, who had befriended him on his arrival, kindly allowed him to stay on in his rented room; but it was an embarrassment to him not to be independent and to have his own home, which he wanted to be in the Chinese quarter of the city.

He wanted to be there because that part of the city was full of sadness. Imperialist troops from the north and rebel forces from the south had wrecked homes, set fire to shops and left gaping holes in the walls where their cannon balls hit. Foul-smelling rubbish piled up on the streets, dead bodies lay unburied and often partly eaten away. The sights were disgusting and horrific even to a medical man. Many people were homeless, wounded or prisoners. This was where help was most needed. Many times Hudson crossed the plank bridge between the Settlement and the Chinese city to bring medical care to the wounded and to give out food supplies to hungry families. What he saw on those visits made him all the more determined to learn the language and to live among the people. This was why he had come, he reasoned, yet every attempt to find a Chinese house had failed. Because of a further battle in which Europeans were involved, non-Chinese were forced more than ever to stay within the safety of the Settlement.

The sun was still quite hot as Hudson folded up his letter ready for posting. He put on his white jacket and tied his black cravat. His search for a house was on again. The unexpected news that a doctor and his family were coming out to join him made him all the more desperate to find accommodation not only for himself but for a whole family. The thought of having company was cheering after six months very much on his own. Those six months had been so trying too. Hours of language study left him with a feeling of being caged in. Mosquitoes bit and brought fever. Funds were never very high. Loneliness made prayer difficult and criticism easy. Now he had the problem of a family coming. He prayed as he walked. He told his Father of his predicament. He would surely find a solution to his problem.

That day near the North Gate of the Chinese city he found just what he was looking for — a twelve-roomed house. To be honest, it was a ramshackle building in a filthy condition which took ages to clean and decorate. The workmen whom he hired for the job slackened off whenever his back was turned, so he took his desk and chair over to his new premises and settled to study in the middle of dust and work.

He moved to his new home at the end of August along with his Chinese helper and language-teacher, Mr Si. It was great to be on his own, he thought, although danger was not very far away. The noise of cannon could be heard distinctly every night. The screams of prisoners being dragged through the streets by their pigtails were sickening and drove sleep away. But he had come to work and he was determined not to let anything get in his way.

He began by opening a day-school for boys and girls. It was really Mr Si who gave the lessons while Hudson listened to their voices chanting out their words. This helped him to get his pronunciation right and every day he felt he was getting nearer to the time when he could make himself fully understood.

He started a dispensary also for there were so many who needed medical treatment. This was one of the best ways to gain the trust of his neighbours and to help them in their misery. Somehow, it helped Hudson to forget his own too, for he was still very lonely at times and had hoped very strongly that a young lady whom he had met in Hull, and to whom he had written regularly would agree to join him as his wife and help him in his work. But she never came.

A short morning and evening service to which all the neighbours were invited became part of the daily routine. Those who could read Chinese shared in the verse by verse reading of the Bible. For a week or two Hudson did not dare attempt to read. But then one morning he took his turn. What a thrill to hear his own voice in Chinese! When he went to make a note of the event in his diary, he discovered to his joy that it was exactly one year to the date after his sailing from Liverpool. Not that he was yet word-perfect, but it was a beginning and he was never again so nervous of meeting people in the market or out on the street.

But generally, things did not become any easier. The fighting continued, very close at hand. There was not much food to be had in the market or in the shops and, as he had done in Hull and in London, Hudson tried to exist on the minimum. He ate only rice flavoured with scraps of pork or vegetables. Soon his stomach was protesting, his body weak and his temper apt to flare up.

He was living in a dangerous place too, and he knew it. At night he kept a small lamp lit beside him and his swimming belt handy in case he had to make it across the ditch that separated the native part from the Settlement. On the one hand the Imperialists threatened to burn out the Chinese quarter, while on the other the rebels had two cannons pointing up the street where he lived.

Winter came with its cold nights, but coal was too expensive to buy. He managed to get a second-hand wood-burning stove and that helped a bit during the day, but at night his two thin blankets hardly kept out the cold draughts that blew through the cracks between the wooden planks of his house. He never had enough money to allow himself any extras yet his Committee at home did not seem to realise the strain under which he worked or the hardships which he suffered. He knew only too well that Dr Parker and his family would be arriving soon, and the more he thought of their coming, the more convinced he was that this house with all its noise, its danger and its fearful sights would never do for a family. He was not sorry that he himself had gone there, but, "Please, God, give me a more suitable house somewhere else for the family" — became his prayer every day. Houses were so impossible to find. What should he do?

One night's terrifying experience at the North Gate House made him pray more desperately than ever. He was awakened by the crackling of wood and the crashing of timber. Snatching his lantern in his hand, he hurriedly climbed on to his roof in time to see a neighbouring house disappear in flames. With the slightest breeze the fire could spread rapidly and get out of control. He fell on his knees where he was and prayed aloud for protection. Bullets were flying in all directions. Some whizzed dangerously near, skimming the tiles. Cannon-balls exploded in great thunderous bursts. Hudson, alone on the roof-top, suddenly felt drops of rain on his bare head! Thicker and faster they came, extinguishing the fire and silencing the night-battle. Hudson left his look-out post, a bit shaken, but impressed by God's ability to answer prayer. He still did not know what to do for the Parkers, but he knew that somewhere God had the answer.

He had. A missionary house back at the London Missionary Society Compound suddenly and unexpectedly became vacant. Would Hudson care to rent it, he was asked? He had to make a quick decision for others would take it if he refused. He paid the rent and went over to collect his belongings from his North Gate House. While he was there, a messenger called to say he was wanted over in the Compound. Imagine his surprise to find the Parkers already there, waiting for him and for the keys to get into their rooms!

CHAPTER SEVEN

Inland China and a frightening experience

THE TWO YOUNG men handing out Christian papers and copies of Gospels from their fast-emptying bags were the centre of attraction. Their western-style dress — black, double-breasted frock-coats worn over white shirts, black cravats held in place by a gold tie-pin, black trousers and leather boots — and their un-Chinese accents brought all kinds of remarks from the friendly crowd that milled around them in the courtyard of the Buddhist monastery. Joseph

Edkins and Hudson Taylor, on his first journey out of Shanghai, took it in turns to explain to these Sung-kiang people the message which they had brought. Faces were upturned in undisguised interest as they told of a God who was loving and fatherly, of Jesus his Son who had come to give His own life for all kinds of people everywhere. Looking down at them all the while was the massive painted dragon on the curved roof of the temple, and all around ugly, fearsome but powerless idols scowled at them from their corners.

Their stock of books had run out and they were just about to move on when several yellow-robed priests with shaved heads pushed their way through the crowd and came up to them.

"Would the honourable teachers care to see our holy man?" they asked.

"Our pleasure would be exquisite," the visitors replied, bowing in the proper manner.

Through dark halls and corridors they followed their guides, their footsteps echoing along the stone passages. Suddenly the procession halted.

"He is in there," said one of the priests, making a sweep of his hand towards the wall.

Hudson looked. All he could see was a small opening where a brick had been taken out. The priest continued to point. Hudson went forward and peered through the hole. There, in the dimness he could just make out the form of an old man, crouched against the back wall.

Hudson was horrified. This poor bundle of skin and bones had been bricked into this tiny cell! He breathed but had no space to move. Food and drink were passed in every day through the slit to him but he lived on in silence and darkness. His was a living death. Joseph Edkins said a few words to him about Jesus in a dialect he could understand. But oh! the feeling of hopelessness they had as they walked sadly away. They breathed a prayer for the 'holy man' as they went back to their hired boat, tied up at one of the landing-stages.

On board they had stored all that they needed for a week's travel on the inland waterways — baskets of food, a stove and saucepans, blankets and bedding, a stock of medicines and a supply of booklets for giving away. It was a thrilling experience for Hudson to get a first glimpse of China beyond the walls of Shanghai. Village after village came into view as they glided along the canals with their brown muddy banks and low-lying green shores. Peasant-homes were poor shacks hardly fit to be lived in, each one with its idols, its paper gods and its incense sticks. Every village had its burial ground where great mounds of earth covered the dead. The heart of the young missionary was deeply touched at these sights.

The call of inland China was growing loud and clear. He prayed that one day he would be able to leave the 'comfort' of Shanghai and go out into that vast land where so many millions lived in superstition and poverty, and so few had gone to tell them about the love of Jesus.

Inland China! Hudson took every opportunity to find out more about it. Once, after days of visiting and giving away books in many villages, when their voices were hoarse with talking and preaching, Hudson and another missionary friend, Mr Burdon, decided to have a day off. They asked their boatmen to leave them at a certain spot where they could climb into the hills overlooking the Yangtse from the north bank. It was a beautiful day with a slight, cooling breeze. They chose the highest peak and began their climb. Gay little flowers patterned the hillside. Trees of many kinds added their colour and perfume to the scene. Here and there amongst the trees, stone steps led the way up to the summit, where a tall square pagoda stood.

A Buddhist monastery and temple spread out and upwards from near the foot of the hill. Curious as ever, Hudson and his friend went inside to have a look. The sight that met them was breath-taking. The interior was magnificently decorated in gorgeous colours. Gilded idols and figures around the walls shone in splendour. Workmen in hundreds were adding more paint and artistry with brush and chisel. It happened to be a day of festival and people of all kinds were there, some in rich flowing robes of finest silk, some very poorly clad, but all intent on their idol-worship, bowing down to their gods, throwing their offerings of coins into baskets and burning paper objects in sacrifice before their gods, while smoke and in-cense-fumes filled the air. The missionaries were filled with sadness.

They climbed on up the slope. The hillside was dotted with many more shrines and idol pavilions to which people had come to worship. What a different scene when they reached the top and stood out on the balcony of the pagoda! Rain had brought life to the countryside and the early crops looked promising. Villages and farms speckled the landscape. The giant Yangtse, more than fifteen miles broad at that point, sweeping on to the sea, was calm and bright with the sails of hundreds of boats and junks. Hudson stood for a long, long time, looking and longing and praying for China.

From the other side of the pagoda they could see the sprawling city of Tung-chow where they intended to call the very next day. Tung-chow, they had been warned, was a city of wickedness. Teachers and servants advised them strongly not to go there, but they saw no reason why they should be afraid, even if it meant suffering for their Master.

Filling two bags with books, they went next morning into the street to hire the only transport available — wheelbarrows and men to push them! — and started off, with one servant, on their seven-mile journey. Mud, rain and potholes made the wheelbarrow ride most uncomfortable, and they had not gone very far when the servant asked to be released from his task. His fears had got the better of him, so he was sent back. But the missionaries carried on.

A little farther along the road a stranger met them, and hearing what their intentions were, said they should definitely go back. The Tung-chow soldiers were merciless and would certainly give 'foreign devils' a rough time. They listened, but decided to go on, singing hymns and quoting verses from the Bible to cheer each other up.

Near to the city they got out of their odd transport and told the wheelbarrow men to wait for them. Then they prayed that God would help and protect them. As they walked on towards the West Gate, they could hear whispers of 'black devils' coming from passersby. They passed several soldiers, who took no notice of them, and were pleased that all was going so well.

All of a sudden a scuffle made Hudson turn around. His friend was struggling with a monstrous, half-drunken soldier and in seconds the two missionaries were surrounded by an angry, swearing mob of soldiers who pushed and jostled them around. The bully of the party soon left Mr Burdon to direct his attentions to Hudson who was much smaller. He seized him by the collar almost choking him, pulled him by the hair, then forced him to walk towards the city with his arms behind his back. Mr Burdon was following, suffering in the same way.

Not knowing whether they were going to be killed or not, they were hurried through street after street. All their protests were useless until Hudson managed to slip one hand into his pocket and pull out an official red card of identity. This saved the situation. Changing course their captors took them slightly less roughly to the residence of the Mandarin, the local government official. There they were left standing with their backs against a wall until their cards had been taken in for inspection.

Feeling sore all over, dirty with dust and perspiration and parched with thirst, they asked for seats and a drink. The answer was no. Undismayed, this did not stop them from preaching to the inquisitive crowd which soon gathered!

After a long wait, word came from the mandarin that they were to be taken to someone of higher authority. The two missionaries immediately refused to go further until sedan chairs were supplied for them. How could they appear at the court of an important person in any other way, they argued. So they were carried there, in style! But, from the appearance of the buildings at which they stopped, it looked for a moment as if they had been taken to some prison. Again their cards were sent in ahead of them and they had to wait wondering just what was to happen. This time the Tao-tai, or chief official of the region, came out personally to receive them and escorted them into a private room. There they were able to explain their reason for visiting the city and they made him a gift of some books. To their joy the governor treated them kindly. First he had tea and rice cakes brought in for them, then he gave them permission to make a tour of the city and hand out their goods. Finally he even sent a soldier with them to guarantee their safety! They left the residence, incredibly happy, to continue their work and then return very tired by wheelbarrow along the bumpy road to their river-boat.

CHAPTER EIGHT

Kwei-hua becomes a Christian

HUDSON LOOKED AT the pile of clothes lying on his bed and had to laugh. This was his new suit, tailor made, Chinese-fashion, but looking a little odd to his eyes.

"Tomorrow will be the big day," he thought as he picked up the baggy knee-length pants and held them against his body. Two feet of extra width would have to be tucked in somehow under his belt. He looked at the hard, cotton jacket and shuddered to think what it would feel like against his skin. As for the shapeless calico socks! They were to hold his breeches down, but how was he to hold them up? He laughed again at the thought. What a freak he would be in his new outfit! Fortunately his heavy silk top-gown was quite a good cover-up for his underthings. But he dreaded the idea of wearing those flat-soled, turned-up shoes which pinched his toes and made his heels and ankles ache. He had already tried them out more than once and was not looking forward to the experience again.

Dr Parker and his family were due to move south next day to Ning-po, and Hudson planned to go with them part of the way. Several months had passed since the missionary group at Ning-po had invited the doctor to take charge of their hospital and he had agreed. The rooms in the Settlement which Hudson and the Parkers had rented and shared together for some months were needed for another family. The problem of lodgings in Shanghai, which had bugged Hudson over the year and more he had been in China, was with him again.

For weeks he had walked the streets of Shanghai looking for rooms to rent. His search had left him utterly weary and depressed. The only thing left for him to do, he decided, was to live in a houseboat, wear native-teacher dress, get accustomed to eating with chopsticks and so improve his language ability and his contacts with the people. This was closer anyway to his idea of what a missionary should do: get to know the local people.

His Chinese suit all in order, Hudson left for the quayside as he had promised to hire a junk for the Parkers and their luggage. But his mind was not so much on where he was going, nor what he was doing, as on a seemingly crazy idea which he had and which would really complete his Chinese disguise. He was toying with the notion of shaving his head and wearing a pigtail! Actually this was not the first time that thought had come to him. In fact he had already taken the trouble of preparing a black dye to disguise his sandy hair and while doing so had been badly shocked and injured when a bottle of ammonia had exploded over him.

A pigtail and a shaved head! The idea was a bit staggering, but now that he was to be so alone, he did not mind too much what others might think or say of him. He walked on, his determination to go the whole way with his latest craze growing with every step.

Stop. A man was bowing to him.

"Would the honourable foreign teacher want a house in the Chinese city? Would a small one of only five rooms be of any use?"

Hudson could not believe his ears. Here was

someone actually offering him what he had been looking for for weeks! It was incredible. The man went on to explain that a friend of his, a house-owner, had found himself in the unfortunate position of not being able to finish the building of his house because his money had run out. But if the honourable foreign teacher so wished, he could have the house for the advance payment of six months' rent, which came to the sum of £10. Hudson clinched the deal on the spot. Within hours of his being homeless, God had come to his rescue and he was full of gratitude to Him. He hurried about his business, went for the key to his new home at the South Gate and, on his way home, made an appointment for the barber to call that evening.

Oh dear! His bald scalp smarted painfully after the barber's razor had finished its work. Spots of prickly heat were cruelly hot but he did not dare to scratch them in case of infection. The fringes of his own hair at the sides and back were pasted up with the black home-made concoction which had to stay on for hours to take effect. That night Hudson hardly slept a wink, and in the morning he had to endure tortures while the barber fixed a false pigtail of plaited black silk into his own hair. Was it worth it, he wondered.

He was almost afraid to step outside. The hot sun was unbearable on his recently-shaved head and he could not cover it as only Muslim men wore hats in summer. People stared at him. Some thought he was a Chinese teacher working for Dr Parker — until they heard them talk to each other in English! But by the time he had left the hired junk and the Parker family and was on his way back to Shanghai, he realised joyfully that he was able to move unnoticed among people. It was not till he produced his bag of books or his medical supplies that they realised who he was, and then he was accepted by them.

Sad to say back in Shanghai things were different. It had not taken long for the news of the young missionary's wild scheme to leak out. Most of the Europeans thought he had gone quite mad and would have nothing more to do with this 'crack-pot fellow'. Even some missionaries felt he had gone too far in copying the Chinese, and they left him severely alone, which made him look for friendship more than ever with the Chinese.

Soon his newly-acquired home at the South Gate in the native part of the city became a centre of activity with school, dispensary and Bible services. People crowded in at the doors to ask his help, filled the rooms to hear him preach about his God, and kept him so busy from early morning till after sunset that he did not have time to be lonely or bored.

When one morning his servant, Kwei–hua, came

to him asking if he could be baptised, he was beside himself with joy. On top of that came another unexpected blessing, a gift of money from a Mr Berger, in England, enough to cover the expenses for six months for the education of Hanpan, one of Hudson's best pupils. That was the second gift from Mr Berger, who for many years afterwards sent money to help him in his work. The Society had failed to look after him properly, but God was never short of people or funds it seemed. The amazing thing was that time and again the gifts from Mr Berger arrived just when Hudson was down to his last pennies.

Kwei–hua was just the first of a number who became Christians while Hudson lived in the South Gate house. As the group grew he began to feel at last that his work, and the painful experiences he had suffered, were worthwhile.

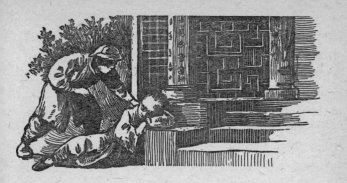

CHAPTER NINE

Poorer than ever

"What do you want?"

Hudson huskily breathed the words out into the night air. The beggar, startled in the act of giving Hudson's body a gentle going-over, grunted something and shuffled off.

"Whew! That was a close one," he thought, letting out a long sigh of relief and gathering the folds of his cloak a bit tighter around him. He shivered. The night was cold, but the shiver was more from fear than anything else. He took his money-bag out from under his head — he had been using it as a pillow — and divided his Chinese cash into piles. Then he hid them in his deep pockets and up his sleeve. He lay down again on the stone steps of the temple and dried to doze off. But he was uneasy and unable to sleep. That beggar might try again, he thought, as he pushed his hands into his pockets. Besides, his mind was still in a whirl after the happenings of the last two days.

What days they had been! After nine months he was on his way to Ning-po again. On the second stage of his journey, his opium-smoking coolies had let him down, refusing to go any further than the South Gate of Shih-mun, and Yoh-shi, his servant, had disappeared taking with him Hudson's precious boxes and bed. His supper the night before had been cold, burnt rice with snake-steaks fried in lamp oil. His feet were now blistered and sore from his trudging in the hot sun all around the dock area of Hai-ning because an informant had lied to him. When night came he was refused lodgings, his 'guide' abandoned him about two in the morning beside the temple and now a robbing beggar had added to his misery!

How far away Ning-po still seemed to the weary and wary traveller! He was on his way, he hoped, to see Dr Parker. The nine months since he had gone part of the way with the doctor, and then had made his memorable debut in Shanghai as a Chinese-Englishman, had been packed with good times at the South Gate house. There had been weeks of exciting medical and preaching work on the Island of Tsungming where a group of new Christians had been formed, and some months with a Scots missionary, Mr William Burns, far south at Swatow. Because he was short of medical supplies Hudson had to come north again to Shanghai, only to discover to his horror that a fire in the London Mission Compound had destroyed all his stocks. The quickest way to get some more, he decided, was to visit Dr Parker and ask his help until further supplies could be sent out from England.

But he was hardly half-way to Ning-po and nothing had gone right for him. He lay perfectly still on the stone step, his eyes shut, pretending to be asleep, but thinking all the time of the scheming beggar. Again he became aware of quiet footsteps coming in his direction, and he felt a hand groping under his head for his money. Without moving an inch, he spoke a few words quietly as before. A shuffle of footsteps. He opened his eyes. *Two* beggars were sitting at his feet!

"What are you doing here?" he asked rather crossly.

"We have come to spend the night too."

"Then kindly move over to the other side of the steps."

They stayed where they were! Hudson pulled himself upright, his back against the wall.

"You know you really ought to lie down and sleep or else you won't be able to work tomorrow!" the beggar's voice was cheeky. "Go on. We'll look after you."

"I don't really want your protection, thank you," Hudson stated firmly. But the men refused to move.

Then a third beggar appeared on the scene and Hudson felt goose-flesh rising. What were they going to do? Three of them could easily overpower him and there would be no-one to help. Again pretending to be asleep, he let his head fall over his chest, but he was really praying desperately that God would protect him from the strangers. Sometimes one of the men would come up close to him — Hudson could feel his warm breath on his face — and look to see if he was sleeping. At that Hudson would say something just to let them know that he was still alert.

At last, he hit on another idea. He would sing hymns! When he could not remember the exact words, he fitted some in, and when his throat felt dry, he quoted some verses from the Bible so that the beggars could get the full benefit. Then he began to pray aloud. That was too much for his tormentors. One after another they slunk away into the darkness. There was even time for a short sleep before the morning ringing of the town bell woke him again.

But he knew that he would have to give up his idea of going to Ning-po alone, and he returned instead the way he had come over the past two days, looking for his missing servant and his belongings. In a tea-shop on the way he learned that Yoh-shi had spent a day and a night with a friend in Shih-mun, but had gone off that morning with the stolen goods saying that he intended to take them to Hang-chow. There seemed to be no point in trying to make up with him.

So Hudson counted his money. He might have just enough for his boat-fare to Shanghai with a very little left for food for the day's journey. He calculated his losses — there must have been £40 worth in the lot that Yoh-shi had gone off with. What a waste of everything in the last day or two! Hudson could not understand why it had all happened. Deep in thought, he crossed the narrow streets from south to north of Shih-mun. He thought for a long time about the life of Jesus, how He had had no real home, very few friends and not much money, how people had treated Him badly and in the end had killed Him. His own losses did not seem so bad after that. He felt ashamed that he had put such value on things.

He felt better when he neared the canal and hailed a passing mail-boat, but it did not stop even when he ran after it shouting loudly in Chinese to the crew. By this time exhausted and very weak, he collapsed by the water's edge, and, if it had not been for the kindliness of a captain whose boat was grounded at the other side of the canal, he might have died there of exposure. The captain arranged for him to be taken on to Shanghai by another mail-boat and offered to pay the shipmaster any expenses if Hudson was unable to do so on reaching the city. It was almost like the Good Samaritan all over again.

So though he was glad to be back in Shanghai, he was poorer than ever. With no money and no medicines, what was he to do? Some well-meaning folk advised him to have his servant Yoh-shi arrested and charged with theft. Instead he wrote a letter, telling him that although he knew of his misdeeds, he forgave him. Hudson was sure that this was the only way to help this man to understand the forgiving love of God. After all, the loss was only of things, and he knew that God would take care of that side of the matter for him.

And so He did. Before the goods had even been stolen, a gift of £40 from Mr Berger was already on its way to him, and it arrived just as he was about to leave once more for Ning-po, 'the city of the peaceful wave'.

CHAPTER TEN

Maria comes to tea

MILKLESS, SUGARLESS COCOA. Ugh! At least it was hot, for boiling water was all that the two missionaries, Hudson Taylor and his friend Mr Jones, could afford. And it helped to cheer them up a little bit.

They had been out all morning in Ning-po trying to find a buyer for their clock, the only saleable article which they possessed for they were completely out of money and food. But the only merchant who fancied the clock wanted to try it out first for a week before handing over the money!

As poor as ever and feeling a bit down in the dumps, they had returned to *Kuen-kiao-teo*, the house and compound which they shared in Ning-po. Fortunately, Mrs Jones and the children were out so they were spared the sad explanations. Mr Jones had been included in the invitation, but he felt he could not leave his good friend in this food-less plight. In gloomy silence they sipped their cocoa and thought through their situation. The sickening thing was that they were expecting two very important visitors for tea that very day — Mrs Bausum and Miss Maria Dyer from the girls' school. They certainly could not cancel that arrangement for Hudson had recently become engaged to Maria who was a teacher in the school.

There, as they sat, right in front of them, above the mantlepiece in the sitting-room, hung two Chinese word-pictures which Hudson had painted while he was in bed ill for almost a month. One said God had been his helper all along, and the other that God would see to all his needs. Their needs were certainly big and urgent right at that moment. Was there anything else they could try to sell?

Of course there was the iron stove, but that was useful. They thought about it for a moment, then decided to hump the heavy thing to the foundry on the other side of the river where they might get a buyer. But when they reached the crossing, they discovered that the foot bridge had drifted away with the tide, and they had no money for the ferry-fares. Even more disconsolately, they carried the clumsy stove back home.

Their Chinese cook, who guessed from the state of the cupboard that funds had run out, offered to help. He had a little cash left from his wages, but the missionaries would not hear of such a thing. Prayer, they knew now, was the only way to change the situation. They went into their study and knelt down to pray, although even Hudson had to admit he did not have much faith that there would be a quick answer.

They had not said very much to God before they were interrupted by an impatient knocking on the door, and an excited voice called out, "Teacher! Teacher!" as the cook burst into the room with a handful of letters. Mail had unexpectedly arrived, and in one of the letters was a generous gift from Mr Berger.

Frantic preparations in the kitchen followed a hurried excursion to the market. By teatime the table was a credit to the quick work of the cook, and who would have guessed the story behind it all? But Hudson could not keep the secret too long. Shrieks of laughter came from the family and the

guests as he related the affair of the clock and the
stove and the tasteless cocoa. Hudson noticed how
happy Maria looked and wondered if he had any
right to ask such a dear, sweet person to marry a
man who was always so poor. Besides, he had no
qualifications like some of the other missionaries,
neither was he very popular with some because he
had gone Chinese. He looked at her tenderly. He
would put the question to her again, he decided,
although the wedding date was only two weeks
away.

By then Maria would be twenty-one, the age at
which her nearest relatives, an uncle and aunt in
England, had agreed she could be married to
Hudson. Her missionary parents had died while
she was still very young and, after schooling and
some teacher-training in England, Maria had
offered to help in the running of the girls' school in
Ning-po. The headmistress, a Miss Aldersley, ob-
jected very strongly to Maria's friendship with
Hudson. She would not allow it to go on until
official permission had been granted by Maria's
guardians in England . . .

Hudson had waited anxiously for long months
for their reply to his letter, and he had been very
ill part of the time. It happened after he had volunteered to nurse another missionary with smallpox. He was up day and night, and it was a terrible
blow to him when the patient did not recover.

Then as Hudson shared the isolation room with him, he was not allowed to leave it wearing his usual clothes as there was danger of spreading the infection. But he had no others! And he had given away a lot of money just a short time before that to help out another missionary. He could not possibly afford to buy a new suit! Unexpectedly a box of clothes, which had been 'lost' on the way from Swatow to Shanghai and which he had given up hope of ever recovering, suddenly turned up. He could appear in public again, much to his relief. But not for long. The ordeal of nursing, the strain of waiting for a reply from Maria's relatives and the fact that he was not allowed to see her brought his health so low that he himself fell victim to the dreaded smallpox . . .

But those tense months were almost now over and forgotten in his supreme happiness — except perhaps for one joyful incident which took place during that time and one phrase which would always stick fast in his memory. Mr Nyi, cotton-dealer, business-man and devoted president of a sect of the Buddhists in Ning-po, had a great interest in anything religious. One evening as he was passing the Jesus' Hall he wondered what was going on, for a bell was ringing and a number of people were turning into the open door. He watched for a second or two, then courageously followed. A young foreigner in Chinese dress was reading from a sacred book. The story was quite new to the visitor. It was all about a holy man who lived many centuries ago whose people had found healing when they looked up at a serpent which he had erected on a pole. Very interesting, thought Mr Nyi. Then the foreign teacher went on to talk about one called Jesus who had been put on a cross. This death, said the teacher, was because all mankind had sinned. That was true, agreed Mr Nyi, Buddhism taught the same. What was the young man saying? That this Jesus was alive? He had come to life again after death? That was what he wanted to know about — life after death. What was that? Eternal life was for all who would believe in Jesus? Those were the words he had wanted to hear for years. That was the truth for which he had been searching. The talk was ended. There was silence in the little preaching hall – until Mr Nyi stood up just where he was and said in a voice loud enough for all to hear, "I have searched for the truth for a long time, but I have never found it. Tonight I find peace in what I have heard. From now on I am a believer in Jesus."

That was the beginning of a new life for Mr Nyi, the merchant. Soon after he asked Hudson how long had the Good News been heard in England.

"Several hundreds of years," he replied.

"What!" exclaimed Mr Nyi. "Is it possible that you have known about Jesus for so long, and only now have come to tell us? Oh, why did you not come sooner?"

The memory of those words lived on ...!

Hudson glanced again at Maria. He loved her very deeply. Could she possibly put up with him for the rest of her life?

Quite simply after tea he put the question to her, and quite emphatically, she gave him the answer that he was the only one she loved and she was prepared to live, give and love as he did.

January 20th, 1858, was the Wedding Day. It was no stylish affair, but the sun shone down brightly on the happy pair, Hudson in his cotton suit and Maria in grey silk dress and veil. The American Consul kindly loaned them his own sedan chair as their wedding carriage and Hudson declared that it was the very nicest one in town.

CHAPTER ELEVEN

Marriage and new friends in Ning-Po

MRS. TSIU CAREFULLY laid her New Testament on one of her brightly-coloured silk squares, folded over the edges and knotted the ends to form a carrying handle. Shutting her door behind her, she stepped out into the Ning-po street and hurried along on her tiny, bound feet to the home of her very old, very deaf and almost blind friend. This little old lady had turned almost everyone from her by her never-ending grumbles and complaints. It was just 'by chance' that Mrs.

Tsiu had found her sitting all alone one afternoon while she was on one of her visits round the court-yards where she talked to women busy with their sewing and read to them from her New Testament.

Not that Mrs Tsiu had been doing this for a very long time. Her son had brought her a copy from the foreigners' house in Bridge Street where he spent most of his days. Then he had persuaded her to let him give her reading lessons. She had laughed at first at the very idea, but he had been quite sure that she would succeed, for this book had been printed in a simpler form than the usual Chinese classic. And he was right. In a very short time she became a reasonably good reader. Besides the more she read, the more she realised that the Jesus' message and the Jesus' way were the right ones. Mrs Tsiu became not only a good reader but a good Christian.

That was why she was sharing her faith with the women of Ning-po, among them the blind old lady whom she was now sitting beside. What an effort it was to make her understand anything! She shouted the words one by one from her book into the old lady's ear. They sat together for ages till Mrs Tsiu finished the lesson by asking her to come to the Jesus' hall where she would meet the teachers and others who were following this way. The old lady agreed – and soon she too began to walk the Jesus' way. In all weathers, rain or cold. leaning her arm on the shoulder of her grandchild, she would trudge the miles to and from the Bridge Street preaching hall.

Above the hall Hudson and Maria had fixed up their home not long after their marriage. They had changed the long, bare, draughty attic where Hudson had lived for some of his bachelor days, and where the snow had drifted in through the gaps in the tiles on to his padded bed-cover, into a cosy flat with dividing walls and locally-made furniture. The ground floor was used, as before, as a dispensary, school and chapel.

But Ning-po had become a town of sadness. China was fighting both a civil and a foreign war. People were on edge because of some dreadful happenings and threats of Rebel invasion. There had been massacres and attempts at poisoning, foreigners were not too popular, and many of the richer people had fled, panic-stricken, from the town. So the young couple did not find their work very easy. Mr Nyi was a gem, so helpful and willing. Mrs Tsiu and her son brought much happiness too. And there were others . . .

Neng-kuei, the basket-maker, was one of Mr Nyi's friends. He was very impressed by what he heard and saw at the preaching hall. The pictures which Hudson used to explain his talks fascinated Neng-kuei, for all Chinese love pictures. When the message began to mean something to him, Neng-kuei became a follower of Jesus. He joined the others in Bible study classes after his day's work was over and, learning there that God had given one day in seven for rest, he told his employer that from then on he would not work for him on Sundays.

"Very well," said his master, "no work, no wage and no food for that day."

Usually food was part of the day's earnings, so now Neng-kuei had to save from his two pence a day to cover his food for Sundays. This came very hard on him, but he would not give in.

It was the busy season for basket-makers when his employer quite abruptly said to him one Saturday,

"You must come in tomorrow to work."

"Have you forgotten our arrangement?" asked Neng-kuei.

"You must come tomorrow, or not at all," the master threatened.

Neng-kuei did not want to lose his job. If he did not obey, he would be sacked. Right then, he *would* be sacked!

Monday morning found him walking the streets in search of a new employer, but not one would have him. How strange, he thought, for he was an expert craftsman and there was plenty of work at that time of the year.

"The devil is having a kick at me," he said to himself. "Well, I'll have my own back on *him* before the day is out. I'll give my time to Jesus and talk to people about Him."

Gossiping in the tea-shops was one of the best ways to spread news around and there was never any lack of listeners. That was where he would go – to the teashops. He took some Bible leaflets with him for those who could read, and was on his way.

He was leaning across a table talking to a group of tea-drinkers when another man joined them. He had been listening at a distance but now was full of curiosity to know more, so when one man slipped away, he took his place. The words he heard absolutely amazed him, Wang, the farmer from O-zi. Surely this was why he had come to town? Ill in his country-home, he had had a sort of vision and was sure he had heard a voice telling him to go to Ning-po where he would hear of a new religion and find peace of heart. Now it was all coming true!

That very evening Wang moved his belongings to the home of Neng-kuei and began his first reading lesson! Before nightfall the two friends had shared their problems and their meal. Wang had learned the first six letters of the alphabet and Neng-kuei had done his work for Jesus very well.

Next morning the basket-maker was out on the street again. This time he found out why no one would have him the day before. His former employer had warned all the other master-craftsmen in the guild of basket-makers not to give workman Neng-kuei a job if he called on Monday. However, this was Tuesday and a good employer decided that he needed a good workman. Neng-kuei had found himself a job again.

So today the basket-maker was almost hidden from view in the middle of his pile of goods for sale. His baskets came in all sizes and shapes, most of them for everyday use and some for decoration. Neng-kuei pushed his way through into the courtyard of a rich family, and all the ladies trotted out to inspect what he had to sell. There was a buzz of conversation and then a voice was heard above the others.

"What! You do not sell incense-baskets? You will not make one for me?" The lady did not seem to believe this possible.

"With respect, ladies, please do not be angry with me," answered the Christian basket-maker, "but I cannot take an order for anything that is used for the worship of idols."

"And why not?" all the ladies asked at once.

"Because I am a follower of Jesus, and worship the only true God," replied Neng-kuei, and then took time to explain his faith to an amazed audience.

Someone had been watching and listening all the time in the background. Wang, the painter, who was doing his work on the ornate ceiling of an overhanging balcony, was fascinated by all he had heard. When the ladies disappeared he came down from his ladder, wanting to know more and Neng-kuei was very willing to tell him. From then on Wang Lae-djun, the painter, became a regular visitor at the preaching services and then a true Christian.

The Taylors' first year at the Bridge Street house was almost over when Maria took seriously ill. Hudson badly wanted to try a certain medicine on her as a last hope for everything else had failed, but he knew that he would have to go over to the hospital and ask Dr Parker's advice first. How hard it was for him to tear himself away from Maria, leaving her alone and so ill. The hospital buildings and dispensary, very recently completed, were right at the other side of town, outside the wall. All the way across, Hudson ran and prayed, asking God to keep his dear Maria alive till he got back. Dr Parker said he should try the medicine and told him what dose to use. Losing no time, he raced back home, to find Maria sitting up in bed and looking fitter than before! By summer a little baby daughter, Grace, was born into the family.

As summer changed into winter a new problem had to be faced. Mrs Parker had died after a short illness and the brave doctor, who had put so much into the setting up and running of the new medical block, decided that it was best that he should take his four children home to Scotland. What was to become of the medical work? The hospital was full of patients and every day there were queues waiting at the dispensary.

"Would you be willing to keep the dispensary open?" he rather fearfully asked Hudson, knowing how full his programme already was. The question could not be answered on the spot. Hudson needed time to think it through and to pray with Maria so that they would be guided by God in the matter.

Surprisingly, they offered to keep not only the dispensary open but the hospital too. Of course it would mean that their hands would be full and the responsibility was quite frightening. But if God wanted them to do this, and they were sure He did, He would help them through. They would have to ask Him for a lot more money to keep things going, they knew, but they were willing to trust Him.

Hudson called the hospital staff together and told them that they had just enough funds to cover expenses till the end of the month. After that they would have to accept whatever God sent. Everyone was given the chance to stay on or leave. Some left. Soon the news of what was happening at the medical centre was heard around town and

Christians offered to help. They volunteered to work part-time, gave some of their money and brought gifts of food, so that there was always enough both for the hospital patients and for those coming to the clinic.

"We have opened our last sack of rice this morning, master," Kuei-hua the cook called out as Hudson was passing on his way to see the out-patients.

"Then, this must be the time for God to do something special for us," he replied cheerily without stopping.

And so it was. Before the last handful of rice had been put into the pot, a letter and a cheque for fifty pounds lay on the office table. The letter, from Mr Berger, promised more money as it was needed for he had just inherited a small fortune and wanted to put it to good use for God. The news of this 'something special' spread like an infection all through the hospital. Staff and patients shared in the thrill, and some, who had never heard of anything like this before, wanted to know what kind of God this was whom the foreigners had brought.

That sense of joy stayed with them all through a difficult winter when there was never an empty bed in the hospital. Some patients had quite tricky operations performed on them and, without much equipment, Hudson's skill was often put to the test. Success brought gladness to many sufferers, but the secret, the missionaries knew, was prayer and trust in God. Day by day they proved this and told the people all around them the Good News. The number of those who took the Jesus' way grew and grew as they watched the lives, and heard the words, of those in charge of the Ning-po medical centre.

Work, work, work. How often Hudson and Maria wished they could be in a dozen places at once. Mrs Tsiu and her son, Mr Nyi and Neng-kuei, and the two Wangs did their share of helping to make the message of Jesus known in the town and in the country villages. But there were still far too few on the job, far too many places beyond their reach and there seemed to be no immediate possibility of help. Worse still, in spite of a short holiday in the hills, the two missionaries were in poor health, worn out and in need of a long break in England. If only others would come out to carry on the work which had become so dear to them . . .

"If I had a thousand pounds China should have it. If I had a thousand lives China should claim every one of them. No, not China, but Christ. Can we do too much for him?" Hudson wrote to his sister Amelia just before the family set sail from Shanghai on the *Jubilee*. On this first trip home they took with them their good friend and servant, Wang Lae-djun, the painter.

CHAPTER TWELVE

On Brighton beach

THE WORD WAS difficult to translate into Ning-po Chinese. He knew what it meant, but the only word he could think of did not quite seem to express the idea. He would have to wait for Mr Gough, another missionary home in Britain from China, to arrive.

Hudson laid his pen down on his desk, pushed the wad of paper from him and took up his Bible to read it. For weeks and months now Mr Gough and he had been working together in the Taylor home in London on the revision of the Ning-po New Testament. They wanted to make the language of it up-to-date and understandable. Mr Gough was an expert in Greek and so he was able to check that the meanings were as near the original as possible. Today he was late, and Hudson was in no mood to concentrate . . .

He looked up at the large wall-map opposite him. There was China — immense, crowded and full of idol worship. Every one of its eleven provinces was clearly named and outlined. He had studied that map for so long that every name was written on his memory — North of the Lake, South of the Clouds, Clear Sea, South of the River, Four Streams, West of the Mountains . . . The great Chinese Empire was forty-four times the size of Great Britain. There were hundreds of walled cities, thousands of busy, bustling towns, tens of thousands of peasant and pagan villages and millions of people. Millions of people, four hundred million they said — the thought haunted him. He imagined a great line of them walking past him single-file. It would take twenty-three years to do it he reckoned. Every day some thirty-three thousand died, a million a month. The thought would not leave him by day, and at night disturbed his sleep. His dreams became nightmares that shook and troubled him — because four hundred million Chinese were living and dying with no-one to tell them of Jesus.

Not that there were not missionaries in that land. There were Americans, French and English and he himself had sent out a few since the family had returned home. But their missionary work did not go farther than the coastal towns — and the need was so great in inland China.

A course in medical studies, so that he could be properly qualified when he did return to China, and the revision of the New Testament, had been two of the ways in which he had personally tried to do something for that land. But more than anything else, Hudson knew that he needed people — God needed people for inland China.

He wrote articles for Christian magazines, he toured the whole of Britain and he tried to use his influence in getting other missionary societies involved — all for the sake of China. People listened to the young preacher and were taken by his enthusiasm and moved by his urgent appeals, but that seemed to be all.

The wall-map kept sending him the same message. He could not escape from it. Along with others he prayed a great deal about China's need, and, through it all, he began to realise that God was asking *him* to head up an advance party into the interior, asking *him* to become leader of a new mission. Could that be possible? He had no money, few friends, little influence . . .

His Bible-reading told him he could not make up excuses. God was a Father who was to be trusted, it said, who gives His children everything they require when they are obedient and goes with them into all the world.

But the idea of starting a new mission, finding a group of workers and seeing that they were well looked after, was almost more than he could face. Supposing no-one volunteered, supposing there were not enough funds, supposing the workers turned against him if an emergency arose in China, supposing? His mind was so full of it that his health began to be in danger.

A weekend at Brighton gave him the break he needed. It was June and Hudson was glad to spend a day or two in the fresh sea air away from the city. On Sunday morning he went to church with his host. The pews were packed, mostly with rich merchants and their families, the men in their well-pressed comfortable suits, the ladies with their billowing, starchy dresses and their picture hats.

The minister, an elderly gentleman, preached a good sermon. The congregation rose to sing the final hymn, a thousand and more voices filling the warm air, and Hudson, a spectator of the scene, felt suddenly choked with a sense of desperation which was almost anger. How could they — so many, so religious, so comfortable, so uncaring? Oh China! He seized his hat and rushed out.

The beach was quiet. All Brighton was at church, it seemed, for that was the fashion. Hudson strolled along kicking thoughtlessly at the pebbles. The sun shone and the sky was blue. Beside him the waves rolled in, crashed and receded. So like his heart, he thought, surging up and down, breaking with love for China.

Did God really mean him to form and lead a group of volunteers for inland China? If one were to die of sickness or famine, what then? The same old questions again! Like some great concrete-mixer, thudding, pounding, churning, they turned over and over in his mind.

He stopped. A word from the morning sermon suddenly became alive.

"If God asks us to do anything, He accepts the responsibility."

The preacher had said something like that. What a fool he had been to worry at all! If God was asking him to take a party to China, to lead a mission, to spread the Good News in the interior, then God would accept full responsibility. He did not have to worry about where the money would come from or what people would say. That was God's affair. He had just to be obedient. His fears and doubts and questions slid like a great load from off his back. He felt free. Taking his Bible from under his arm, he opened it to where he had been reading that morning and wrote:

"Prayed for twenty-four willing skilful labourers — Brighton, June 25th, 1865."

He had reckoned that number as the minimum to start off with so that every province should have two missionaries and two for Tibet. As he prayed he felt a deep-down peace that God had heard him and would answer that 'absurd' prayer.

He was so sure about it all that, two days later, back in London, he opened up a bank account in the name of 'The China Inland Mission' with the only ten pounds he possessed as a first deposit. It was a start, only a small beginning, but then every great work for God has a small beginning. He knew only too well that to run a mission *that* amount would have to be multiplied many thousands of times over. Somehow it did not bother him! As to how it was all to happen, how he was to recruit men and find money he did not have a clue. But he knew it would happen in God's way and in God's time.

The walk along the Brighton beach had done him a world of good — not just the fresh air and the sea-breezes which he had enjoyed, but the new sense of God's being in charge which had come to him. He knew he could go on from there.

Prayer had been his habit for a long time, but

mostly for himself and his own affairs. Now with things developing, could he trust God and prayer alone? Yes, he would. God could and would make people willing to go and to give. He made up his mind that he would not appeal for money, not try any profit-making dodges, but just talk to God about everything ... Men, women and money began to trickle in ...

From rich and not-so-rich, from Liverpool and Dublin, Aberdeen and Oxford came gifts, cheques, a printing press and medical equipment. Most important of all, came people, volunteer missionaries from all over Britain and one from Switzerland. The Taylor home was a centre of activity and training. When one house became too small for the enlarged family they moved to another and saw God supply the increased rent.

A certain colonel had organised a meeting for him. The wealthy audience was fascinated by the young man's story, the details and descriptions of life in China. They could have waited longer to hear more. At the end someone suggested that a collection should be taken up.

"No, no. Go home, all of you. Ask God there what He would have you do about China. Perhaps it is you He wants, not your money," was Hudson's unexpected reply.

Later that day, the colonel protested about his action.

"With all those people there, you could have had a good collection," he grumbled. Hudson would not listen.

Breakfast was delayed next morning as the colonel had not appeared. As Hudson waited in the hall, the post arrived, bringing a letter from a shipping company who offered places for all of the seventeen people who were then preparing to sail — eight had already gone to Ning-po — on condition that £400 be paid in advance. £400! The bank balance for the China Inland Mission did not nearly come to that amount. Would God do something special that day?

The colonel was at the door, excusing himself for he had had a bad night. The reason? The thought of China's millions had troubled him, kept him awake, made him pray. The result? He had handed it to Hudson in the form of a cheque for £500!

Twenty-four willing and skilful labourers was what he had prayed for on the Brighton beach that Sunday morning in June. By May of the next year Maria and he with four children were leading a party of fifteen new missionaries on board the three-masted windjammer, *Lammermuir*. What a mixed bunch they were — a blacksmith, a merchant's daughter, a governess, a carpenter . . . But they had much in common — they loved God, they wanted to serve Him and they were headed for China trusting Him to help them all the way through. And others were preparing to join them later that year.

CHAPTER THIRTEEN

Typhoons and Troubles

BUT THE VOYAGE to Shanghai was almost disastrous. Little volcanoes of annoyance erupted between members of the missionary party leaving hurt and confusion strewn around. At one point the crew threatened mutiny and the captain suicide. Two terrible typhoons battered the ship pitilessly until finally with broken masts, ripped sails and exhausted crew she limped, a wreck, into the Yangtse channel and had to be towed by steam-tug up the Woosung Creek. Hudson could hardly be blamed for wondering if he had made a big mistake.

There was no welcoming party waiting for them on the shores of Shanghai either. Instead — only horrid, snobbish gossip and unwillingness to help. No European would give accommodation to a crowd of seventeen adults and four children. They had not been given warning of their coming, they said. And what right had Hudson Taylor to bring out so many at once, amongst them unchaperoned single girls? Such unheard of behaviour! The inhabitants of the exclusive International Settlement would have nothing to do with the new-comers.

But to Hudson's joy one missionary, an American, did understand their plight. He opened up his home to them and put their boxes into his baggage-store. There, for about a week, they sorted out their gear, cleaning and repairing, washing and repacking it, for the salt water had seeped into the packing-cases and the hampers. Meanwhile Hudson busied himself in town. He filled up forms for passports for the interior, ordered Chinese clothes for all his company and made arrangements with the barber to shave the heads of the fellows and fix them up with pigtails.

The International Community was in an uproar. Taylor was a ridiculous crank, a misguided fanatic, a madman, the wagging tongues said. The Press took over, reporting his actions, twisting the facts, making headlines out of minor details. It took a brave heart to deal with such opposition, and Hudson's faith and courage were pushed to their limits by these bitter attacks on him. Outwardly, it was 'business as usual' for he planned to move with his missionaries into the interior as soon as possible.

The map of China was still firmly in his mind, and so now was his programme for advance. The capital city of every province was to be tackled first. Then, when they had gained the support of those in highest authority, they were to use that as a lever to open up new centres in the chief cities of the prefectures or divisions of provinces. When work there was going well, they were to start in the smaller towns.

One of the conditions for the success of such a project — (one which was quite obvious to Hudson and Maria if not so to all the others) — was that they should all adopt the Chinese way of living. Hudson had not come to China with any westernised package of Christianity to hand over to the Chinese. He looked forward to seeing 'Chinese Christians, truly Chinese in every right sense of the word ... worshipping God in their own tongue and in buildings of their own style.'

So while bald heads still smarted from the

barber's razor and Chinese dress made walking awkward, they boarded three canal boats which were to take them south to Hangchow, the capital city of Chekiang.

But the journey was a slow business. For more than a month the weird, Chinese-looking, English-speaking company lived on their narrow floating homes, cramped during the day while trying to do language-study and chilled by the penetrating cold of the November nights. Hudson could sense that his team had good reason for complaint and he found it difficult to cheer them on. But he then remembered what God had said to him on the Brighton beach and knew that *He* was in charge.

Hangchow, once a vast, prosperous city lying mid-ways between Shanghai and Ning-po, had suffered under rebel fire and many parts of it had been reduced to ruins. The house which Hudson found to rent was a great, rambling building, once the home of an important mandarin. There were rooms upon rooms connected by dingy passages, space enough for all the 'family' and to spare for offices, dispensary and classrooms. But it was in a terribly bad condition — somehow that never bothered him — and a few families still lived in parts of it. But at least it allowed them to start in one of the capitals of a province, and that was according to plan.

"Go around quietly until the people get used to us being here," Hudson warned his workers. "Get acquainted first with the neighbour-families and then gradually appear in public." Foreign teachers had come to their city, and for the Hangchow Chinese, who had every right to be suspicious, that could mean trouble.

At mealtimes some of the more curious neighbours would stand about shyly looking on, taking note that the foreigners had only simple wooden benches, plain board tables and native-made beds. They sat around bowls of hot, steaming rice and ate somewhat amateurishly with chopsticks. Perhaps they were not too queer after all, they reckoned.

Hymn-singing and prayers in Chinese brought a friendly crowd into their meeting-room, and by the first Christmas in Hangchow the missionaries had organised a regular Sunday service. Oh, not at all like an English one. People came to listen, but only to listen would be a waste of time. Some of the women brought sheets of silver paper and sat making 'money' out of it (to be used for burning in their idol shrines) during the service. It was not unusual for some to take out a pipe and have a few whiffs while the Bible was being read. And if a man brought his dog to church, well, what of it? Sometimes the message would be interrupted by a question from the audience and could continue only after a good answer had been given.

Soon all Hangchow knew that the foreign teachers had come to bring very special news and to be friends. Hudson, as usual, made a quick start with medical work and all too soon had more patients than he could reasonably cope with. About two hundred of them with all sorts of complaints passed through his surgery every day and often several members of a family would come together. Street-sellers made good profit out of the surgery-queues by taking up their stance nearby. Hudson loved his work, every bit of it, not only when doctoring and advising, but even more when preaching to the crowd which swarmed daily into the courtyard to hear about Jesus' way.

From Hangchow, where next? The plan had to be carried out, and Hudson himself led the survey team which went out into the country looking for new centres from which they could work.

A married couple was sent to Siao-san along with Tsiu, the evangelist. The townspeople eyed them suspiciously for the rumour was that foreigners stole away Chinese babies at dead of night, killed them and pickled their bodies! And when the foreign-teacher-man appeared on the streets, not in his Chinese clothes, but in western dress, the people were panic-stricken. They were sure that something dreadful was going to happen.

They held a council of war, stormed the mission house, filled the downstairs chapel-room, seized Tsiu and called on the missionaries to appear. When they did, they were roughly treated, brought before a magistrate and, without being allowed to say a word in self-defence, they and their foreign religion were attacked. At the command of the official, Tsiu was severely and brutally beaten hundreds of times on the back and then rolled over to suffer repeated lashings on the chest and face. In fact his life was almost beaten out of him.

Hudson was shocked when he saw him. Good, hard-working Tsiu had been so wrongfully punished and the cause had mostly been the foolishness of the non-Chinese missionary. As their mission leader, he was deeply hurt and begged the missionaires in Siao-san to put their Chinese dress on again. They refused and soon, others of the group were influenced by them and followed their example. This kind of opposition from within the team came hardest on Hudson. How could he ever hope to open up inland China with his forces split down the middle? God had to stand by him in his moment of crisis and remind him that He was still in charge as He had promised to be. But it was the moment his critics were waiting for.

"Told you so," they said cockily, and their words hurt.

"Just as I said — no good would ever come out of that hair-brained missionary's plans," seemed to be the usual kind of gossip in the Shanghai circles.

The slanging tongues were at it again and the newspapers were not slow to take it up, in China and in England.

Well, let them. It hurt a lot. But Hudson had set a standard — become Chinese to win the Chinese for Jesus Christ — and he was not going to change. If he gave in to other people's gossip now, he was sure of only one thing — failure. He was determined to go on as planned.

CHAPTER FOURTEEN

"Kill the Foreign Devils!"

JUST WHERE THE waters of the Grand Canal and
the swirling Yangtse River meet, lay the city of
Chinkiang. A bustling and busy trading-port, it
seemed just the right place to open up one of their
first mission centres. So Hudson enquired about
premises inside the city. As the ones he wanted
were not then vacant he set about filling up forms
and papers in the hope that there would not be too
much delay. Meanwhile it seemed pointless to

wait around, so the group moved on to find another place further north.

Yanchow was on the north bank of the River. With its turretted walls and its splendid buildings, it was a city inhabited mainly by the rich, the retired and the scholarly. It allowed little of the outside world to disturb its calm. Its most famous governor had been the explorer, Marco Polo, in the thirteenth century.

After a great deal of bargaining and endless discussions, the Taylor family, their missionary colleagues and a few Chinese servants managed to find an innkeeper willing to rent them five rooms in the upper storey of his building. This was certainly better than crowded living on leaky junks in the rainy season and so they happily moved into yet another temporary home.

Yangchow people were not much different from Hangchow people. They were curious, in need of medical help and made good listeners. After six weeks at the inn, the missionaries had the promise of a house in the town. Besides, it seemed as if the Chinkiang house would soon be theirs too, and Hudson intended to have the mission printing press set up there.

Suddenly illness struck – not for the first time. One of the servants became ill and they were afraid it might be smallpox. Naturally Maria hurried off to Shanghai to have their baby girl vaccinated. Sadly their oldest daughter Gracie, had earlier died of a sudden illness. Then, while they were away, Hudson went south to Chinkiang to see about the house affair and became so dreadfully ill there that he could scarcely make it back to Yangchow. As soon as the news of his illness trickled through to Maria in Shanghai, she rushed with the baby to find a river-boat, but all she could hire was one with a single oarsman. In her desperation to get back quickly she hired the boat and took turns with the man at the oars so that no time would be lost.

How glad she was to be back to care for the ones whom she loved so intensely! How good to get things straightened up in their new home! But not for long. Horrible stories were being spread around the town. The foreign doctor (Hudson) took people's eyes out to make medicine of them, it was being said. Chinese priests, afraid of losing their followers, fanned the flames of rumour into a wild fire of fear and superstition. The more educated Chinese accused the missionaries, behind their backs of course, of being in conspiracy with the British Government. They said that the missionaries were involved in a plot to reduce China to a state of weakness through the opium trade. And over in Chinkiang all kinds of excuses were being hatched to keep them out of the house which had already been signed and paid for.

Tempers rose even higher when five boat-loads of printing press, intended for Chinkiang, came on to Yangchow. As crate after crate was seen being carried into the mission building, suspicions ran high. What were the foreigners hiding in those boxes? The townspeople could only make a wild guess — and they thought the worst.

The very next day an unsigned letter addressed to Hudson arrived at the house warning them that an attack was about to be made. A little later stones came crashing through the windows, frightening the children. Hudson reported the matter at once to the chief town official, but he paid no attention.

A second letter came. The missionaries put up barricades, prayed and waited. For almost a week they were under siege, the angry mob coming and going, sometimes violent and brick-throwing, sometimes ready to listen to a quiet talk from one of the missionary men who dared to go out and face them. At the end of a week, things had quietened down considerably and it seemed that the danger had blown over.

Then two visiting Europeans from Chingkiang, having heard of the trouble, decided to come and check for themselves. This was the last straw. Their very European clothes in an anti-foreign atmosphere sparked off trouble. They had hardly left the town to return south when a great shouting and wailing was heard in the streets, "Twenty-four children are missing ... twenty-four children are missing ..." Of course the children were safe but there could be no mistaking the ugly mood of the people, ready to find any excuse for trouble.

Angry and out for blood, and carrying flaming torches they rushed on the mission house, frenzied and screaming, "Kill the foreign devils! Kill the foreign devils!" They battered at the doors and barricades throwing stones and bricks at the wooden window-shutters.

Indoors the missionary family prayed and handed themselves over to God's keeping. They were trapped and at the mercy of the mob. As calmly as she could, Maria hurried the children upstairs into bed and the other women joined her while the men stood guard by the doors and windows. The mounting din outside was frightening enough but they all knew that, worse than that, the crowd would eventually break into their home.

Hudson wondered what he should do, not for himself, but for those for whom he was responsible. So although it was a pretty risky idea that came to him, he had to take that risk. He suggested that under cover of darkness he should try to reach the official residence and there ask for soldiers to quell the riot. On hearing this, one of the young fellows volunteered to go with him. Together they slipped out into the shadows, made their way through the neighbouring courtyard and headed across the fields. Unfortunately they were spotted running and a group of fellows joined in the chase, their voices filling the night air.

"The foreigners are fleeing. After them!"

Stones came flying at them. They were struck on their legs, but they sprinted on in an all-out effort to reach the residence. With not a scrap of energy left they arrived at the gate to find it slowly closing on them. Frantically they flung their weight against it. It swung open again and they fell flat on their faces in the courtyard. Picking themselves up, they shouted at the top of their voices,

"Kiu-ming! Kiu-ming!" which means 'Save life!' for they knew that the official would have to appear at their call for help.

Meanwhile back at the mission house things became more and more terrifying. The rioters broke down one of the courtyard walls and surged forward. They tore at the barricades and pushed their way into the ground-floor rooms. Just in time, one of the men missionaries managed to get up the wooden stairs to the women and then fasten down the trapdoor. A few moments later the ground floor was ablaze.

Then began a desperate escape operation. There was one missionary left down below, and he rescued the children as they were lowered out of a window, over a ledge and on to the ground. Then he hurried them off to the shelter of an outhouse. During one of his absences, someone lit a brushwood fire under the ledge making further escape almost impossible. But the ladies bravely jumped for it and all but Maria and another had escaped when the trapdoor was forced open and a brute of a man stepped into the room. He roughly handled the two women, tearing from them any articles of value he could seize.

Then he turned his attentions to the missionary who was helping the escape on the ledge outside. He dragged him down by his pigtail and a struggle followed. Hoping to distract him, the missionary threw his watch out into the darkness. This only maddened the fellow who tried to force the missionary backwards over the ledge then picked up a brick to bring it crashing down on his skull. Fortunately the women were too quick for him. They grabbed his arms just in time. He swung back into the room and did them no further harm, concentrating on joining the looters who were swarming everywhere.

There was no time to lose. Maria was last to jump and she hurt her back in the fall. Limping and bruised, they at last found the shelter of the outhouse and from there they managed to creep to the safety of a friendly neighbour's house, leaving their burning home to the plundering mob.

At the residence, Hudson and his friend were almost out of their minds with impatience, waiting for the official to put in an appearance. When he did, he seemed little concerned at what was going on and in no hurry to help. First, he said, he must really know what had happened to the 'missing' children. What had Hudson really done with them? His talk was exasperating beyond belief.

Worst of all, now and then the wind blew the shouts of the crowd through the night air to the residence. The missionaries could only make wild guesses at what might be happening, and what they imagined was horrible. Were the women being tortured or the children being put to death? At a moment when time was so important, why did this official persist in foolish talk? At last the official left the room, saying he would see what could be done, adding casually, "Twenty thousand rioters are out tonight. Yes, we had better get them quietened, then we can talk."

Two hours of awful suspense went by. Hudson and his friend felt like bursting through the doors to get out again. Imagine the relief when an army commander appeared with the official to tell them that the trouble was over and that they were to be allowed home under military escort!

But they were sick inside with fear and horror as they came near the ruined mission house. Not a person in sight! Not a sound to be heard! Only smoke and the smell of smouldering material. Could it be of human bodies? They shuddered. Scattered all around were the bits of broken and charred furniture, books partly destroyed by fire or torn to shreds, personal belongings ripped apart, toys and precious medical kit absolutely ruined. The sight was terrible, heartbreaking. But where were all the members of the family? The agony was almost too much for Hudson.

At last he found them all, still alive, but in great pain and suffering from shock. One had a badly cut arm, another was faint from loss of blood, and all were stiff and sore from knocks and bruises. Gently he led them back to their deserted and almost unrecognisable house, thankful just to be alive. Although the damage was bad, rather miraculously the most important personal papers were safe.

When morning broke, a few stragglers dared to come obviously after more loot, but a group of soldiers sent to protect the family chased them off. That same day the missionary family quickly packed what belongings they could save and sailed over to Chinkiang so that the house could be repaired and the bad feeling allowed to settle.

CHAPTER FIFTEEN

The severest test of all

AFTER ALL THAT had happened many people
would have given up. But his plan for China was
never very far away from Hudson's thoughts, and
kept him pressing on.

The sequel to the Yangchow riot was almost
worse than the event itself. British officials took
the matter up in Parliament, gunboats were sent
in and the whole affair became front-page news.
The struggling group of missionaries wanted only
to forget about it and get on with their job. But

everywhere they found that people took sides for and against them. Those who never had liked Hudson and his methods had plenty to say. The amount of money sent from home dropped because of this, but Hudson braved it all and went on to set his sights for further advance.

But crisis followed crisis, and the Taylor family had their very big share of trouble. Another of their little ones died and the others had to be sent off to England to be cared for, except the baby. There was a great deal of sickness among the other missionaries too, then came the threat of war and rumours of more killings. By far the worst moment was when Hudson had to cope with one of the severest tests of his life. His greatly-loved Maria, only thirty-three years of age, died. Yet again he proved that God is to be trusted and he found Him very near and very real in his loneliness.

Despite all the setbacks he carried on, and on his next visit to England, when he remarried, he reorganised the affairs of the Mission which was steadily growing in numbers. When he and his wife returned to China he toured round all the stations which had been recently opened and were making progress but finding problems.

In Ching-hsien, for example, the centre of a very populous district, some very wonderful things had been happening...

Mrs Nying peeped into the room where her

husband was busy reading a book which he had
brought home that day. She could not understand
why he refused to look up at her or answer her
when she told him how late it was. Hour after
hour this scientist and Confucian scholar read on
in the New Testament which he had been given.
He had told the missionary only that day that he
did not believe in a living God, but the missionary
had just asked him to take the book and read it for
himself. Now he could not put it down; it held him
like a magnet. More than that, he knew that he
was beginning to believe what this book said. But
to be a Christian ... Oh, that was a bit too much.
He would be ignored by his family and relatives;
probably his wife would leave him and take the
children with her. What should he do? What
should he say? He knew that the truths of this
book had completely won him over. How could he
ever tell this to his wife?

"There is something I would like to tell you," he
said at last to her one evening when the children
were all in bed. She waited patiently for him to
explain, but he could not find the words to say. He
hedged for a day or two until she could stand it no
longer and asked him point-blank what was on his
mind.

It was difficult for him to get started, but then it
all came tumbling out — how he was sure now
that there was a living God, that there was no

need of temples or idols, that there was a way of forgiveness through Jesus Christ. To his surprise, his wife was taking it all in without a question and becoming very excited about it too! She had something to tell *him*, she said, something which had happened to her many years before . . .

When she was a little girl, the rebel army had come into their village. The soldiers, for no reason at all, had marched into the houses of the people, wrecking, robbing and setting them on fire. Many of her relatives had been killed. Terrified at what was going on all around her she had crept into a wardrobe in one of the rooms to hide. She heard the sound of heavy boots and knew that the soldiers were in the very room and their loud voices frightened her. But she lay very quietly and prayed,

"Heavenly Grandfather, please save me."

The soldiers moved off and she came out from her hiding-place. Ever since then, she said, she knew there must be a living God but she did not know how to find Him or believe in Him.

Mr and Mrs Nying began to share their new-found faith with others in the town. The mayor was most upset when Mr Nying told him about Jesus, and reported him to his superior at the University. But Mr Nying witnessed to him too. There was just no stopping him. In fact the 'terror of the town' was one of the first to become a Christian and the change in his life was so great that others followed his example, his own father being one of them. The owner of the gambling-hall was another, and before long the shutters went up while the hall was redecorated for use as the preaching chapel.

How glad Hudson was to meet with this group of new Christians on his journeys, to hear what God had done for them and to share their joys.

Hudson's visit made it clearer to him than ever that Interior China — 'the great Beyond' — was in need of more workers. Chinese evangelists would have to be trained and many more missionaries sent out from England. They would have to be men of courage and stickability for the job was tough. Shirkers and cowards would be of no use at all. Maybe he should try out some of the new arrivals to see if they would make the grade!

It was very early on a cold November morning. Hudson put on his quilted suit and covered his head and ears with the wind-hood. All that could be seen from this ball of padding was his nose and mouth! He lifted his Chinese umbrella, a huge affair which he carried handle-first, before going out into the street to hail a wheelbarrow-driver to take him to the docks.

The young men at the dockside who saw this 'Chinaman' approach on his wheelbarrow got the shock of their lives to discover that he was their leader! After introductions, he invited them to his 'hotel' and to them the prospect of a bit of luxury-living was rather pleasant...

It was a long walk past the foreign settlements, into the native suburbs. Where was he taking them? He stopped in front of a post office, opened the door, crossed through to the other side, opened another door and then climbed a dark stairway which led into a small square room, very barely furnished and rather dismal, for the only window space was covered with a grimy piece of paper. A wooden table, a food-basket in a corner and some boxes covered with rugs was the furniture — and this was the 'hotel'. They were not impressed!

Hudson asked them to sit down. Then, taking his Bible, he read from it and talked to them about the passage which they had read. They were impressed!

Would they like to wash before breakfast? That seemed a fair enough question but where and how? There was no sign of a bathroom anywhere. Hudson went to the door, called out something in Chinese and a man appeared. He bowed to the visitors, took a wooden bowl from the basket, laid a small sort of face-cloth on the table and went out. He was back in a few minutes with the bowl full of steaming hot water which he had obviously gone out to buy.

Carefully he placed the bowl on the table, dipped the face-cloth into it, wrung it out and handed it to Hudson who wiped over his hands and face and gave it back again. There was a second dipping and wringing a little bit tighter this time and a second rub-over for Hudson. The young fellows looked on in amazement, and then it was their turn to go through the procedure.

"Now, let's go and have breakfast," their leader said to them without giving them an inkling of what might be on the menu.

Hudson led them through the busy streets, stopping at several cook-shops to enquire if they had what he wanted to order. At last he found a suitable place and they went in. They perched on very narrow forms while the waiter dusted over the table and set down chopsticks for each one. Then he brought in four bowls of rice and vegetables and a bowl of chunks of fat pork. With a twinkle in his eye, Hudson chose out the biggest lumps for the new-comers and kept piling them on top of their rice till they had to ask him to stop. It was just too much. But they had passed their test and Hudson was pleased. He and China could do with many more of their kind.

The thought of the nine provinces still without missionaries troubled Hudson constantly. But the strange thing was, when he most wanted to be around and open up new areas, he was taken seriously ill and forced for weeks to do nothing — or so it seemed. But they were weeks

when talking to God became more real than ever
and, by the time he was well enough to get about
again, he knew that God had spoken to him about
starting a Western Branch of the Mission. It
seemed such foolishness just then even to think of
such a project for he was so weak, funds were so
low and there was a lot of sickness in the ranks, but
a letter arrived at that very time with a promise of
£800 to be used only in advance work. That made
him quite sure it was God's plan.

This seemed to be the repeated pattern of his
life. Hudson, always keen to be on the move for
God, would find himself ill and weak. Then God
would show him how he should pray, how the
work was to go on, and he would be back on the
job as soon as health allowed it.

There was the time while travelling on the
Yangtse that he slipped from the top step down
the gangway of the cargo-boat and fell heavily. A
sprained ankle and a painful back crippled him
for days, but when he arrived home in London
some time later his legs crumpled under him and
he was temporarily paralysed from the hips. It
was bed once more when there was so much to be
done, but from his few square feet of space he
wrote about China's need and prayed for eighteen
new workers for that land. No less than sixty
offered! In later years the same kind of praying
was done — for seventy workers, for a hundred

and even for a thousand and every time God answered prayer.

Once when he was on board ship on his way back to China he became very ill and the doctor was all for putting him ashore at Hong Kong. But a letter from Mrs Taylor who had been in the interior, helping in famine relief and working hard to establish an orphanage, brought him the unexpected news that she would be in Shanghai. He was determined to go on. Besides he was full of plans for visiting the many stations which had been opened in his absence and giving what help he could. Thirty-four new missionaries had been sent out while he was in England and he longed to be in the thick of things again. It was so exciting to know that so much was happening — churches were being founded, evangelists were in training, medical work was making great progress, so was teaching and preaching.

But he was an ill man, and even in Shanghai, the loving care of Mrs Taylor and all the joy he was having were not enough to bring him back to health. He could not possibly travel to the interior in his condition. He would have to go north to a quiet place by the sea — Chefoo.

The tang of the sea-weed, the pleasantness of the hills around the bay, and the peace he enjoyed on that first visit set him thinking of the future usefulness of such a place. Who would have imagined then that a whole centre would eventually develop on that very site — holiday homes for wearied missionaries, a hospital, and first-class schools for the education of missionaries' children.

Weakness, prayer, faith and action was the pattern again. Of course it took many years to happen — from the buying of the first bean-field from a local farmer, and the getting of timber for beams and cupboards from ships wrecked in the bay to the finished buildings, but God was in the project as it took shape.

CHAPTER SIXTEEN

"The man who brought good to Inland China"

WHEN GOD IS in a work it goes and grows. This is what Hudson found as time went on and his programme took him not only backwards and forwards to China but to America, Australia and New Zealand, to France, Switzerland and Scandinavia. Writing books and articles for magazines, speaking of China at meetings and conferences, visiting people and places were all part of his busy life. Many students in universities and colleges heard the call of God to serve Him in China and in other lands. People from all over the world gave sums of money to help with the work which was making steady progress.

Have you ever seen the tiny trees which grow up around a big tree? Seed-pods have fallen and taken root and they, in turn, become trees of the same kind. So the China Inland Mission which started off as a very small tree, became the parent-tree from which several other missions grew. The best-known perhaps is the Worldwide Evangelisation Crusade whose founder, Charles T. Studd, was one of the students who volunteered for China and served there for a term with the China Inland Mission.

When Hudson was quite elderly and frail, God gave him a home in Switzerland. It was while he was there that some terrible things happened in China which caused him great sorrow.

The nation of China was in a state of unrest. There had been war with Japan, and the country itself was divided by rival parties. The young Emperor was deposed and his stepmother, the Dowager Empress took over control. She, and her supporters, called Boxers, bitterly hated all foreigners and, in an attempt to clear the country of them, she had a public notice displayed in every town of any importance. She stated that all foreigners were enemies of the regime and therefore should be destroyed. The Boxers lost no time in

putting her words into action. They began a cam-
paign of killing and destruction. Missionaries
were forced from their homes. Churches and
chapels were burned down. Property was stolen
and many Christians, both Chinese and foreign,
suffered terrible losses and many were done to
death. The China Inland Mission had a death-toll
of fifty-eight missionaries and twenty-one children.

The news was almost more than Hudson could
bear. How he longed to be back in China where he
felt he belonged and where he wanted to bring
comfort and help. But, slipping on the pine-
needles in the woods near his home in Davos, he
twisted his back and was a cripple once more.
Another forced rest, but his Swiss home became a
centre of prayer as visitors from all over the world
made their way to visit him and share in his
interests in China. Hudson prayed fervently that
he would be allowed to see that land once more,
but that was not to be until he had said a final
goodbye to Mrs Taylor and laid her body in the
churchyard of La Chiesaz, not far from Blonay
Castle.

Then he was able to visit China again. The welcome he got was tremendous. Everywhere he
travelled people turned out to see the man who
had worked so much for them, to shake his hand,
to tell him how much they owed to him. They

showered him with kindness, preparing special meals for him, organising public meetings at which he was honoured and coming for miles just to see and listen to the one whom they lovingly named *Nui-ti en-ren*, 'the man who brings good to inland China'.

Chang-sha, capital of the province of Hu-nan, was one of the farthest inland cities for which Hudson had prayed for many years. Beautifully situated amongst the mountains, river and plain, it had become the centre of widespread medical missionary work and the reports which he had read had thrilled Hudson very much. Now, at last, the moment had come for him to see for himself.

Travelling through the mountain passes from their outpost came a young Chinese evangelist and his little wife to meet the great man of whom they had heard so much. It was Saturday afternoon when they arrived at Chang-sha and as Hudson was having tea with other guests, they thought it best not to disturb him. They would see him at the Sunday morning service when he was scheduled to speak to all the Christians who had come in from the surrounding area.

That very evening, after darkness had fallen, the young couple learned to their sorrow that Hudson had gone quickly and quietly to be with Jesus. They had come a long way to see him.

Would they be allowed just to look at him, they asked, and they were taken into the room where he lay.

What they said then to him, just as if he could hear them, is exactly what many thousands of others from China's Far Beyond would say too,

"Dear and respected Pastor, we have come to see you. We too are your little children. You opened for us the way to heaven. You loved us and prayed for us for many long years. We do not want to bring you back, we shall come to you. You will welcome us one day."

P.S.

One day a little girl who lived in Cambridge decided that she would like to write to Hudson Taylor. Here are some of the words which she carefully wrote out for him,

"Dear Mr Taylor,

If you are not dead yet, I want to send you the money I have saved up to help the little boys and girls of China to love Jesus . . ."

Hudson treasured that letter and used that gift.